Walking Down the Warwick Road
By
Dennis Platt
ISBN: 978-1-9997646-4-7

Second Printing: 2024

Copyright 2024

All rights reserved. No part of this publication may be reproduced, stored in a retrieval system or transmitted in any form or by any means, electronic, mechanical, photocopy, recording or otherwise, without prior written consent of the copyright owner. Nor can it be circulated in any form of binding or cover other than that in which it is published and without similar condition including this condition being imposed on a subsequent purchaser.

The right of Dennis Platt to be identified as the author of this work has been asserted in accordance with the Copyright Designs and Patents Act 1988.

A copy of this book is deposited with the British Library

Published By: -

i2i
PUBLISHING

i2i Publishing. Manchester.
www.i2ipublishing.co.uk

Foreword

Everybody has memories of their childhood, it seems schooldays, more than any other, will never be forgotten.

Upon leaving school you go on to search for a career, find a partner and start a family.

It is not until your children leave home to start a life of their own, that you have more time to think about those early childhood years. Your long-term memory will recollect those early years. Times when all you had to think about was playing out and having fun. Your parents would deal with any problems life could throw at you.

On the other hand, your short-term memory sometimes leaves a lot to be desired. Things you did last year are often hard to recollect. How many times have you gone upstairs and then forgotten what you went for?

If you could imagine your brain as a wastepaper bin which is full to the top with paper; if you continue placing paper in the bin, it will just fall out. Think of that paper as your short-term memory. Whilst the paper at the bottom of the bin is going nowhere, just like your long-term memory.

This book is going to take you back to the 1960's when things were very different from today. From the moment you were conceived, many obstacles would stand in the way of progress.

During pregnancy, many women would smoke cigarettes and drink large amounts of alcohol. Their diet included sandwiches covered in beef dripping, brown sauce, or sugar. Cow heel soup was another favourite meal. They would eat the traditional English breakfast, all cooked in lard.

Once brought into the world, the home environment was not the safest of places. Asbestos was present in a great many homes, and lead-based paint was commonly used throughout the house, even on children's cots.

There were fire hazards present, with open coal fires, and over-loaded electrical sockets. Medicine bottles were stored in the kitchen cupboard next to items such as Alka-Selzer and Milk of Magnesia. Child proof lids on medicine bottles were unheard of.

At school, the teachers would punish you for misbehaving by hitting you with a cane or slipper. Sometimes they would even throw the blackboard duster at you. A smack to the back of the head was not unheard of. This was also what would happen if a policeman caught you misbehaving, which I experienced personally.

These were the days when parents would tell you to ask a stranger if help was needed crossing a busy road. Today children are told not to talk to strangers.

Health and safety procedures were rarely adhered to. Cyclists did not wear head or body protection. Car drivers did not wear seat belts, and building workers did not deem personnel protective equipment a necessity.

Home life could be quite tedious, not all had a television set, and even less had a telephone. On the rare occasion, a telephone call was necessary, it was made from an outside box.

If food items were required, it was necessary to purchase them before 6.00 pm, because that was when all shops would close for the night. On a Wednesday, they only opened for half a day and would not open at all on a Sunday.

The only take-away food available was from the fish and chip shop, there were no McDonald's or KFC.

Many people are too young to remember times such as these. But please read on and try to imagine what times were like, all those years ago.

For those of you who can remember the old, cobbled streets, frozen jubilees, Wimpy Bars, Green-Shield stamps, and 'The Man from the Pru.', let us take a walk down memory lane, to what would eventually become known as 'The Swinging Sixties'.

Chapter 1

Springfield Lane

As I looked at my mother, I could see that she had found true contentment in what she was doing. In fact, she was undertaking a labour of love.

She was kneeling by our front doorstep, a bucket of water by her side, and a donkey stone in her hand. She would dip the stone into the water, and then rub it over the step.

This was a ritual performed by many women of this era. Even through the austere years since the end of the Second World War, people would take great pride in the appearance of the home.

The donkey stones were originally used in factories to create a non-slip surface on the steps. They came in a choice of colours, such as brown, beige and white.

Our stone was obtained from the rag and bone man. You could hear his shouts of 'rag bone' as he went around the streets in search of old clothing and bric-a-brac. He would use either a horse-drawn, or hand cart to convey his daily collections. In return for any items, he would give you a donkey stone or a balloon on a stick. Needless to say, my mother would always choose the donkey stone.

I stood there for a while, watching my mother create this non-slip surface on our doorstep. But I knew it would soon be the time for me to go indoors for the night. For that reason, I decided to move a distance away and join my friends for a game of Tiggy-off-the-ground. But soon afterwards my mother shouted for me to come inside.

It was at this point in time, I was about to make a very bad decision. I decided that I would ignore her and carry on playing with my friends. Not only that, I turned to my friends and gave a wry grin. I thought to myself that at her age there was no way she would come up the street after me. In fact, my mother was only thirty-two years old, and she soon came up the street, grabbed me by the shirt collar and frogmarched me home, lifting me over the front doorstep, and into the house.

This incident will be remembered by me for all time, as it was my earliest childhood memory. As a seven-year-old boy, it taught me never to underestimate anybody.

The scene of the incident was outside Springfield Lane Buildings, Salford, in 1962. The buildings sat in between two factories and a metal scrap yard, just on the outskirts of Manchester town centre. I lived there with my mother, father, and my older brother. Or if you were to say it in the local dialect, 'I lived there with me mam, dad, and our kid.'

These buildings consisted of two-bedroomed flats, with a lounge, which was also the kitchen. The gas cooker and stone Belfast sink were in the same room. Oilcloth covered the floor, with a carpet in the centre of the room. We had a brown leatherette settee, adorned with brass studs. The black and white television set, which stood in the corner, was rented on a weekly basis.

There was no bathroom, and the toilet was in an outside building. This outside building also contained piles of coal, which were used for the open fire.

The rag bone man, with his horse and cart, fully loaded with the day's collections.

One luxury household item we did own was an electric washing machine. This particular one had an electric mangle attached to it. This would squeeze excess water out of the clothes after washing. Prior to this it would have been done by hand.

When my mother was outside, me and our kid would thread newspaper through the mangle. This was until one day I did not let go of the paper in quickly enough. The mangle began pulling my arm through until sticking at my elbow. At this point it carried on turning taking some of my skin as it did so. Luckily my mother heard my cries for help and came in to turn the machine off.

Needless to say, we never touched the machine again. I still have the scar on my arm to this day.

The type of dwelling we lived in had been built by the railway companies in order to house their workers. My father was one of those workers, employed as a shed man at Trafford Park railway sheds. His job was to load the steam trains with coal in readiness for their next journey.

Like most workers of this era, he would travel to work by bus. Unlike today, the majority of people did not own a car. Each day he would leave for work carrying a small bag which contained his lunch. When he returned home his bag would still be full. Only this time it contained a large piece of coal wrapped in newspaper.

During the summer months we would not use much of this coal, but we had a bountiful supply for the wintertime. Although it did begin to get a bit tight for space in the toilet.

The first school I attended was Sacred Trinity, then moving on to St Mathias situated on Great Clowes Street. The classrooms seemed to be enormous, probably due to the fact the desks were quite small. The tiny desks had a slot for pens and a hole for an ink well. To fill the well, powdered ink would be mixed with water.

There were playgrounds to three sides of the school and a gym on the top floor. In the gym there were wall bars, a pommel horse, and thick climbing ropes hanging from high level.

In the playground the favourite games played were tiggy 'it' and British bulldog. The cries of British bulldog, one two three, could be heard when another victim was caught. There seemed to be an endless number of games that we could play.

These buildings on Oldfield Road were similar to Springfield Lane Buildings.

There was a hill behind our school, which we nicknamed the diggle-daggle. During our dinner break we would play there. We would widen our scope and play games such as hide and seek, cowboys and Indians, or king of the castle. This game required the chosen king to climb on some high ground then call out:-

'I'm the king of the castle'
You're the dirty rascals'

At this point everyone else would try to remove him from his elevated platform. These sorts of games were a bit too rough for the girls. They preferred to stay in the playground and play games such as hopscotch, skipping, or simply doing handstands against a wall.

Each day, when school had finished my mother would meet me outside the school gates. Then we would take a longer route home via the shops on Greengate. Britain was known as a nation of shopkeepers, and there was a wide variety there. There were newsagents, butchers, grocers, ironmongers, handyman and hobby shops.

Because many more people smoked cigarettes than they do today, there were tobacconist shops selling many different tobacco products. Wool shops were also common. Women loved to knit items of clothing.

A visit to the butchers shop usually ended up with my mother purchasing tripe and cow heel. The tripe would be eaten cold, accompanied by onions and vinegar. The cowheel was used to make soup, and I detested both of them. If you will excuse the pun, to me they were offal.

I much preferred the visit to the newsagent's shop, for as well as selling newspapers, it was where my mother bought her cigarettes. It would be Woodbines for herself, and Park Drive for my dad. These could be purchased in packs of five, ten or twenty. If money was in short supply, you could also buy them singly. They also had a good selection of sweets. The penny tray was my particular favourite. On the tray were flying saucers, gobstoppers, fizzers, toffee necklaces, and liquorice, which we actually called spanish. All of these were a penny each, but for the same penny you could have four fruit salads, mojoes, or blackjacks. If money was in short supply, we sometimes would have two of these sweets for a half-penny. The farthing was discontinued the previous year, or it might have been one of those sweets. On the other hand, if my mother was flush, a packet of spangles, at threepence was a possibility.

Ice cream could be bought from the horse drawn street vendor. The man making a purchase is wearing a donkey jacket, which was common in this era. Also note the ornate leaded window above the ice cream cart.

After helping my mother home with the shopping, I would go straight out to play. Staying indoors wasn't an option, as there were no computer or video games to play on, and the television programmes hardly inspired the imagination. There were only two channels to choose from, ITV and BBC. Which could be chosen by turning a dial on the TV set to either number three or number nine.

Children's television programmes included the likes of Animal Magic, Blue Peter, Crackerjack, and the westerns: The Lone Ranger, and Maverick. The adults seemed to be catered for better, with programmes such as 77 Sunset Strip, The Avengers, Danger Man, Dixon of Dock Green, and Perry Mason. Comedy programmes included I Love Lucy, The Arthur Haynes Show, and The Benny Hill Show.

As a lot of people did not have a television set to watch, they would make do with listening to the wireless. The cost of a licence for the wireless was £1 per year. But once again the choice of programmes was limited. Children would listen to The Clitheroe Kid, Children's Hour, and the record request show, Children's Favourites. For the adults there was The Billy Cotton Band Show, Music While You Work, Workers Playtime and Housewife's Choice.

But another reason for not watching the television was that my mother said that I would get 'square eyes' if I watched too much of it. Little did I know that was only one of the many sayings my mother would come out with. If I stood in front of the television, she would say 'You would make a better door than a window.' On asking where my dad was her reply would be, 'He's gone to see a man about a dog'. Or if I happened to leave a door open it would be, 'Was you born in barn?' But the one that amuses me the most was when I heard her talking about a neighbour who was cross-eyed, she said, 'She skens like a basket of whelks.'

Many people will be unfamiliar with the currency mentioned earlier. The next chapter should help, in some way, understanding the 'old money'.

In the News

The Sunday Times launched a new venture. It became the first newspaper to appear in two parts. The familiar black and white version, together with a full colour magazine supplement.

Some of the sweets available in 1962.
Left to right: Sherbet Lemons. Dolly Mixtures. Pontefract Cakes. Rhubarb & Custard. Imps. Kendal Mint. Torpedoes. Pear Drops. Sherbet. Polo. Candy Sticks.

A Penny Tray, containing: Spanish. Bubbly. Flying Saucers. Fruit Salads. Black Jacks. Toffee Necklace. Liquorice Wood. Gob Stoppers. Fizzers.

Top:- Another view of Oldfield Road Buildings.

Bottom:- A typical cobbled street of the early 1960's.

Chapter 2

Pre-decimal Sterling

Pre-decimal money had a long history, dating as far back to the Norman Conquest of 1066. At that time the Normans were using their own French coins, which were embossed with a little star, known as esterlin. The English equivalent of esterlin was the word sterling, which then became the name of our new currency.

The small coins kept their original name of one penny. The coins were quite heavy, two hundred and forty being a pound in weight, and so became one pound sterling.

The currency was referred to as LSD, pounds, shillings and pence. The L came from the Latin word libra, a pound in weight. The S and D came from the Roman coins, solidus and denarius.The written form of this money would be £-s-d, the £ merely a fancy L.

The table below shows the money in ascending order.

Farthing, 1/4d, four equalled one penny.	0.1p today.
Half Penny, 1/2d, two equalled one penny.	0.21p today.
Penny, 1d, twelve equalled one shilling.	0.42p today.
Threepence,3d, four equalled one shilling.	1.25p today.
Sixpence,6d, two equalled one shilling.	2.5p today.
Shilling, 1/-, twenty equalled one pound.	5p today.
Florin, 2/-, ten equalled one pound.	10p today.
Half Crown, 2/6, eight equalled one pound.	12.5p today.
Ten Shilling Note, 10/-,Two equalled one pound.	50P today.
Pound Note.	

There was also a crown coin, (5 shillings or 25p today) but it was fairly heavy, and rarely used. The farthing was discontinued in 1961, but there were still a few in circulation.

Over the years the money adopted various nicknames. The half penny was sometimes referred to as ha'pence or hapeny. The penny was called a copper. Threepence was called a threpney bit or thruppence. Sixpence was referred to as a tanner, and the shilling, a bob.

Although there was no coin for two pence, if something cost this much it was said to be worth tuppence. The ten-shilling (50p) note was referred to as a ten-bob note. The pound note was known as a quid or a nicker. The five-pound and ten- pound note were known as a fiver and a tenner, as they are today.

Although the term quid is still used today, there are no other nicknames for money. But they may develop as time progresses.

There were many sayings involving the old money. For instance, if you were to say, 'I'm going to spend a penny,' It would mean that you were going to use the toilet. This was because public toilets could only be accessed by putting a penny in the lock.

If somebody turned up like a bad penny, their presence was not welcome. 'A penny for your thoughts,' is what was asked if you were caught deep in thought.

'Look after the pennies and the pounds will look after themselves.' This meant be careful with your money, no matter how small the amount. If you were prepared to go all the way in a situation, you would say, 'In for a penny, in for a pound.' If an item was said to be not worth a brass farthing, then it would be virtually worthless. When you didn't have two ha'pennies to rub together, you didn't have any money. But on the other hand, if you were 'quids in,' you were very happy with your financial situation.

There were also many songs that mentioned money, such as: -

> Christmas is coming, the goose is getting fat.
> Please put a penny in the old man's hat.
> If you haven't got a penny, an ha'penny will do.
> If you haven' got a ha'penny, a farthing will do.
> If you haven't got a farthing, then God bless you.'

All of the coins were embossed with the head of the reigning monarch. The way the head faced changed each time the monarch changed.

This can be seen in the photograph of the coins below. It can also be noticed that Queen Victoria has a small crown, whereas the others do not wear a crown. The photograph shows two versions of the Queen Victoria coin. The lower coin being known as the bun penny.

From left to right the monarchs are Victoria, Edward V11, George V, George V1, and Elizabeth11.

There were also two versions of the George V coin, his head being smaller on the later coins. On these second edition coins the head would face the same direction.

The missing monarch on the photograph is Edward V111. This was because he was only King for a few months and was never crowned. He had become the uncrowned King after the death of his father, King George V on 20th January 1936.

Edward fell in love with commoner, Wallis Simpson, and in order to marry her, he abdicated on 11th December.

Edward married Wallis Simpson on 3rd June 1937. Once he had given up his throne Edward was given the title of The Duke of Windsor, and Wallis became known as The Duchess of Windsor.

In 1962 the average wage for a manual worker was £15. Not a great wage by today's standards, but the cost of living was very different then. The average house price was approximately £2,670.

Comparing other items to today's prices, twenty cigarettes would cost 25p, a litre of petrol 2.4p, a pint of milk 3p, and a loaf of bread 6p.

It is not surprising today's items cost much more, as inflation has risen twenty-fold since 1962.

Chapter 3

Boom Time Britain

During the 1950s many people in Britain had experienced great poverty. The nation was still recovering from the war, with food rationing still in force up until 1954. As a result, many families were unhealthy and living in squalor.

As the 1950s neared an end, there was a gradual improvement in living standards. But it would be a couple of years into the 1960s when there was a boom in the economy.

At this time everything seemed to improve drastically, gone were the Victorian attitudes of the previous decade. Families found themselves with much more money to spend than ever before. The industry began to thrive, and people could now start putting money aside for items that would previously be considered a luxury.

The average home now contained more luxury items than ever before. Not only did we have electric fires and irons, but we could now afford televisions, vacuum cleaners, electric washing machines, and refrigerators. Also, telephones were much more commonplace, although you may have had to share a party line.

People still had vivid memories of the hard times that had gone before, those previous years of struggle would never be forgotten by the British people. People were still suffering, both physically and mentally, with evidence all around us of the damage and destruction inflicted during the Second World War.

These ruins would become the playgrounds for my generation of children.

There were many outside games children would play, all passed down from elder brothers and sisters. Games such as 'Kick-Can,' 'Follow my leader,' 'Robbers Knock' and ' Rally-vo' were all favourites. If you had to leave the game unexpectedly you would put your thumbs up and shout 'Bellies.' Some of the more sedate games were Conkers, Marbles, and Jacks.

As the streets were virtually traffic free, our parents would allow us to play out for hours on end. Occasionally it was necessary to go home and have a minor wound treated. This was usually done with a purple-coloured antiseptic called Iodine

When teatime arrived, everybody had to go home. These were the days when all the family sat around the dining room table and ate together. After tea we would 'Side the table.' That would mean clearing the table and then play out for a little longer.

A typical street in the early sixties. No cars can be seen.

There were however certain places our parents would not allow us to venture nearby. One was the River Irwell, which flowed a hundred yards from our home. Like all rivers it was much too dangerous a place for children to be near alone. Another place was Greengate, a busy main road running across the top of Springfield Lane.

To deter us from going up to Greengate, my mother would say, 'Don't go into Greengate, or else the Scuttlers will get you.' The Scuttlers my mother referred to were gangs of youths who had roamed the streets at the beginning of the century. These gangs from different areas of Manchester would arrange to meet and do battle on the streets and crofts. They would be armed with knives, iron bars, or anything they could lay their hands on. Their favourite weapon was a thick leather belt with a large brass buckle.

They would swing the belt above their head and reign down blows on the opposing gang members. Inflicting terrible injuries with the brass buckle.

The local Scuttlers would often meet up in and around a nearby public house named the 'Bull's Head,' situated on Greengate. The 'Bull's Head' was reputed to be one of the first public houses in England to receive a drinking licence. It was originally built around 1350, partly of the traditional cruck construction. This involved using naturally curved timbers to support the roof area. This method of building certainly stood the test of time. In 1356 it was granted a drinking licence and became a popular hostelry for the people of Salford and visitors to the city.

The 'Bull's Head' on Greengate.

At that time Greengate was a rural area. The 'Bull's Head' stood opposite a village green. Here stocks were erected to punish any wrong doers. Bear dancing also took place on the green.

The 'Bull's Head' closed for the final time in 1931. It was badly damaged by fire a few years later, and subsequently demolished. Being situated on one the main roads into Manchester city centre, many people would have popped in for some liquid refreshment. Possibly some of the famous people from Salford's past?

One of these people could have been William Crabtree, born in the Broughton area of Salford in 1610. He was educated at Manchester Grammar School and went on to be a successful cloth merchant. His principal interest was astronomy; he would spend many hours observing the planets and stars. Whilst collaborating by post with Jeremiah Horrocks, they worked out the courses of Venus, Earth and the Sun. This enabled them to calculate the 'Transit of Venus.' This was when the planet Venus passed directly between the Earth and the Sun. Their work together was very important in the study of the movement of the planets. This being even more remarkable, as it is possible that the two men never actually met.

One of the other Salfordian visitors could have been The Reverend

William Cowherd, founder of the Bible Christian Church of Salford in 1809. He preached to his congregation to abstain from eating meat. This request was not hard to agree to, as most of his congregation could not afford to purchase meat. After William's death in 1816 vegetarianism grew in popularity and the potato pie became one of the favourite local dishes.

It was also in this era that James Prescott Joule was born. In fact, it was in 1818 that he began his life in New Bailey Street, Salford. A keen scientist, he established the theory of thermodynamics. This theory would show that when force is applied to an object, heat is produced. Thus, the unit of energy, the 'Joule' was now born.

Moving on into the twentieth century, in 1903 Walter Greenwood was born in Ellor Street, Salford. This area was known locally as 'Hanky Park.' Whilst out of work he wrote the novel 'Love on the Dole,' from which a film was later produced. Much of the novel was written in the Ashfield Labour Club, which once stood a few yards from my present home.

The book was written during the depression of the 1930's, and it would show the destructive effects poverty would have on the people of Salford. It described how the community would rally together and overcome their adversities.

Another Salford lad with an interesting life story to tell was James Henry Miller. Better known as Jimmie Miller, he was born in 1915 at Andrew Street, Salford. After leaving school he worked in a factory, but his main interests were singing and writing. He would later develop strong communist views, bringing him to the attention of the authorities.

He went on to marry Joan Littlewood, and together they set up various theatre groups. But at one of their performances the content was deemed inappropriate. They were subsequently arrested and charged with disturbing the peace and were bound over for two years.

Later Jimmie changed his name to Ewan MacColl. He then wrote a play called Landscape and Chimneys, which contained a song about Salford.

<u>Dirty Old Town</u>
I found my love by the gasworks croft
Dreamed a dream by the old canal
Kissed my girl by the factory wall
Dirty old town, dirty old town

Heard a siren from the docks
Saw a train set the night on fire
Smelled the spring of the smoky wind
Dirty old town, dirty old town

Clouds a-drifting across the moon

Cats a-prowling on their beat
Springs a girl in the street at night
Dirty old town, dirty old town

I'm going to take me a good sharp axe
Shining steel tempered in the fire
We'll chop you down like an old dead tree
Dirty old town, dirty old town
Dirty old town, dirty old town

It was around this time that this time that Ewan divorced Joan and married Jean Newlove. The marriage produced two children, Hamish and Kirsty. Kirsty would grow to be a famous singer in her own right.

In 1956 Ewan met American performer, Margaret 'Peggy' Seeger. He wrote a song for her called 'The First Time Ever I Saw Your Face,' which she used in one of her performances.

Ewan and Peggy began to perform together and would become lifelong friends. Eventually they would marry and have three children together.

Below are a few more famous people, all born in Salford:

Composer: Peter Maxwell Davies.
Actors: Robert Powell, Albert Finney, and Christopher Eccleston.
Musician: Allen Clarke from the Hollies.
Footballers: Eddie Colman, Geoff Bent and Paul Scholes.
Singer: Elkie Brooks.
Artist: Harold Riley.
Television presenter: Tony Wilson.

<u>In the News: April 1962.</u>
James Hanratty is hanged for the A6 murders, but many people believed him to be innocent. However, a DNA test in 2002 was to prove Hanratty's guilt 'beyond doubt'.

Chapter 4

Moving House

It was now time for us to move to a new home. A bigger home, closer to my father's workplace was required. All our belongings were neatly packed into a large removal van and off we went.

The term flitting was often used to describe a move to a new home. But that phrase was more fitting to someone who would move quickly from one place to another without staying anywhere for long.

Our route would take us along Chapel Street, and this is where a very interesting history lesson would begin. Our driver was quite an expert in the history of Salford.

Chapel Street was unique, in that it was the first street in the United Kingdom to be lit by gas light in 1806. It was also a part of the A6, a major road that stretched from London to Glasgow.

Our first point of interest was the site of the old Flat Iron Market, which stood in front of Sacred Trinity Church. This church was the first one ever built in Salford, in 1635. The name of the market derived from the triangular plot of land on which it stood. This was because the shape of the land resembled the shape of a flat iron, which was used for ironing clothes. The market closed in the 1930's.

203a Chapel Street was once the headquarters of Vimto, the world-famous cordial drink. It was whilst based at these premises that Vimto was first registered as a drink in 1913.

A little further on was Islington Park, which was once the home of Frances Hodgson Burnett. Frances was the author of the children's classic, The Secret Garden in 1911.

On the opposite side of the road is Bexley Square. The square gained notoriety in 1931 as the scene of the infamous 'Battle of Bexley Square'. Violence erupted during demonstrations by over 10,000 people against government cuts to benefits and the general injustice to the working-class people.

Further along the road we approach the magnificent building of St John's Church. Better known as Salford Cathedral, it was architecture at its best. Built to the cruciform design, or the shape of a cross, it had a splendid central tower and spire.

On the opposite side of the road, we then pass the memorial statue of The Shouting Soldier. Erected in memory of the people from Salford who lost their lives in the Boer War. Many of those who died were Lancashire Fusiliers who had volunteered for service. The statue was unveiled by King Edward VII in 1905 and stands directly opposite Salford Royal Hospital.

The 'Shouting Fusilier' statue.
This photograph was taken many years ago, but I am not sure on what date.

We next arrive at Salford Crescent, which had been built in a similar design to the great Crescent of Bath. The second public house on the left was called the Red Dragon. Aptly named as it was once the favourite drinking establishment of Karl Marx and Friedrich Engels.

Whilst living in London, Karl would visit his close friend Friedrich, and they would deliberate over their book 'The Communist Manifesto.' Although an extremely intelligent man, speaking many different languages, Friedrich subsidised his passion for politics by working in his father's factory.

Next, we come to The Police and Fire Station buildings, which stand directly opposite Salford Museum and Art Gallery. On the lawn in front of this building stand two great statues of Queen Victoria and Prince Albert. These statues were sculptured to commemorate the royal visit of 1851. During the visit a choir of over 80,000 school children sang for the couple.

As we crossed over Windsor Bridge, first to come into view was a red granite obelisk. This was a memorial erected in honour of Salford born, Oliver Heywood, who had performed much work for the local community and various charities.

Sited behind the memorial was The Windsor Theatre. Originally, The Royal Hippodrome, it opened in 1904 and became known locally as 'The

Hipp'. Many famous film stars had appeared there, including George Formby, W C Fields, and Gracie Fields. There were also appearances by artistes, who would become popular on our television screens, such as Tommy Cooper, Hylda Baker, and Roy Castle.

In the centre of the photograph is the Oliver Heywood memorial.
To the left can be seen the Windsor Theatre.

As we turned into Cross Lane we were met by a myriad of shops, public houses, and buildings of interest. On the right stands a covered market, with an impressive clock tower and circular shaped office building at the forefront.

The market site was once home to another distinctive clock. The clock stood on top of Parr's Bank which stood in the centre of Salford Cattle Market.

At one time this market was one of the biggest in England. It also housed six slaughterhouses and sold all types of livestock, until closing in 1931.

Continuing along Cross Lane we came to Lyon's Ice Cream factory, and directly behind it was a funfair. On the fair there were many exciting rides, such as the waltzers, bumper cars, speedway and the big wheel. You could buy candy floss, hot dogs and hamburgers from mobile stalls.

This was all getting too much for a seven-year-old boy to take in; was this utopia? I think my dad was thinking the same thing, only for a different reason. We had only travelled three hundred yards, but had already passed eight pubs.

Moving on, we soon arrive at the Carlton Cinema, the most modern of many cinemas in Salford. The Carlton was built with an Italian theme, inside there was a carved scene of Venice, including a gondola.

Opposite the Carlton stands Cross Lane Drill Hall. Now the headquarters for the local Territorial Army, it was originally the home of the Lancashire Fusiliers. The building has a fort like appearance including a circular turret. Soldiers were sent from the hall to fight in the Boer War and the first World War.

Across the railway bridge is Cross Lane Railway Station. Originally named Cross Lane Bridge, the station was one of many on the Liverpool/Manchester railway line founded in 1830. The station closed in 1959.

Further on we come to Disc City where you could buy vinyl records, or even borrow them if you preferred.

Opposite this shop was The Palace Theatre. The Theatre started life as The Regent Theatre and Opera House in 1901. Famous stars to appear there were Harry Houdini, Josef Locke and Frank Randle. Unfortunately, the theatre was badly damaged by fire ten years ago and is now awaiting demolition.

Next to the theatre stands The Ship Hotel, which is the seventeenth pub on this half mile stretch of road.

In its heyday Cross Lane would have been a hub of activity, attracting many visitors including sailors from the nearby docks. This created a cosmopolitan feel to the area which led to it being given the nickname 'The Barbary Coast'.

In The News

John Glenn became the first American to be put into space. He was picked up from the sea off Puerto Rico after travelling three times around the earth.

Top: A view along Cross Lane. On the left is The Buck Hotel, Fred Oddie's butcher shop, and Jone's chemist on the corner of Liverpool Street.

Bottom: A view in the opposite direction. The photograph was taken outside Fred Oddie's butcher shop on the corner of Liverpool Street. The Carlton Cinema can be seen on the left.

Top: A photograph taken from Cross Lane railway bridge. On the left can be seen The Falcon beer house. Further along is The Barracks with fort like tower.

Bottom: Cross Lane Railway Station, now closed. On the right can be seen Myrtle Terrace, home to my aunt and uncle. In the background is The Station Hotel.

Chapter 5

West Wilton Place

Our new home was to be a two-bedroom end terrace house situated in one of the small, cobbled streets off Cross Lane. There were four streets in this quiet area, situated adjacent to The Carlton Cinema. 22 West Wilton Place was now our new home. The other streets were Jo Street, Myle Street, and East Kirkham Street.

Most of the homes were owned by the Railway Company and rented out to their employees.

This catchment area seemed to have everything we needed. There were numerous shops for my mother to visit, there were many children of a similar age to me, and with the house being a lot closer to my father's workplace, we began to settle in very quickly.

The house was still quite small. From the front door, a lobby led firstly to a front room, named the parlour. This room would rarely be used, the main living area being the back room.

The back room contained the television, the dining table, sofa, and the gas cooker. The floor was covered in oil cloth, sometimes called lino. In the centre of the room was a piece of carpet. There were not many homes which had fitted carpets, known then as wall-to-wall carpet.

Next to this room was the scullery, which was only just big enough to house a stone sink, or as my father called it, the slop stone. The scullery led out to the backyard. This area contained the metal rubbish bin. This was the only bin, unlike today where many homes have four. There was nothing to be recycled then, and many things were burnt on the fire. The metal bin would be collected weekly. The bin men would open the back gate leading to the entry and carry your bin to the other end of the street. Whereas today, even old people have to put their bins out for collection.

The back yard was also the home for the toilet, although this time we did not have to share the space with the coal storage. There was a separate room, with its own door for the coal.

The coal would be delivered to the front of the house and tipped down a hole in the pavement covered by a metal grid. This hole led to the cellar, from which my father would move the coal to the back yard.

The cellar also contained the tin bath. As we did not have a bathroom, the bath would be brought up from the cellar and placed in front of the coal fire. The lighting of the fire was a tedious affair, but my father was an expert. First of all, he would roll up a double page of newspaper and tie it in a knot. A few of these would form the base of the fire, then on top of the paper was placed some coal. There were of course easier methods of creating a base for the fire, such as fire-lighters or bundles of wood, but my father's method was cheaper. Once the paper was lit, the fireguard, or a shovel would be placed in front of the fire and a double newspaper page placed in front of it. This would cause air to be drawn in through the bottom grate, thus establishing the fire. In the meantime, pans of water would be boiling on the cooker in readiness to fill the bath. It was no wonder we did not have a bath daily.

We would also use Pendleton Swimming Baths, or as we called it then, Pengy Baths. Before entering the pool, we had a good wash, which also acclimatised us to the cold water we were about to enter. At the baths everybody wore the same purple knitted trunks, with a string tie.

We would also visit the baths with our new school, Christ Church, New Windsor. The school was quite small, and it was situated in a street off Cross Lane opposite the Market. Often when my mother met us after school, we would call at the Market. While my mother was shopping, we would collect chicken claws, with which you could pull the dangling tendons and make the claws move.

It was then back home to share the claws with our friends and play some of the new games we had learned. Games such as 'Kick Can' and 'Rally Vo'. In order to decide who was 'on' in these games, counting out rhymes were used, such as: -

Eeny, meeny, miny mo, put the baby on the po
When he's done, wipe his bum
With a piece of chewing gum.

Or

Hip dip, my blue ship.
Sailing on the water.
Like a cup and saucer.
Egg shells, you are it.

Cross Lane Market, with impressive clock tower, and circular shop below the market offices.

Our new surroundings also meant many new adventures. If the May Day Parades were on, we would walk to Chapel Street to watch them go by. On the way there we would stop off at the cut canal under Windsor Bridge, armed with our fishing nets; many a stickleback would be caught. On the way back home from the walks, a visit to Peel Park was a nice detour. There we could play on the swings, spider's web, wedding cake and slide. Before we left the park, sticky bobs would be collected. These were in fact Thistle Pods, which could be thrown at each other and would stick to clothing.

As the summer arrived, so did the hot weather. In the cobbled streets the tar, or pitch, would bubble up in between the cobbles. Things to do seemed endless, from playing with cap guns, catapult, or 'gat', to making wooden stilts, or even constructing a bogey. The bogey was made from a wooden plank, some old pram wheels, and pulled, or guided along by a piece of rope. Other areas of England called this mode of transport a guider.

The main play area for the bogey would be the croft which occupied three sides of the Carlton Cinema. This area was also our cricket and football pitches. As it was now summer, cricket was the game in favour. The wickets would be chalked on the wall and as in the rules of the game there were various ways of being called out. The standard rules for being bowled or caught out had a few more connotations, such as if the ball was to hit a wall, it had to be caught with one hand. You were also out if you were to hit the ball over a backyard wall. This rule also applied to the Cattle Dock wall.

The Cattle Dock was where animals were unloaded from trains in readiness for their journey to the abattoirs. From here they would be herded through the streets to Sherlock's abattoir on West High Street. Sometimes a cow or a sheep would make a bolt for freedom. The drovers would then make chase and bring them back to the herd.

Sheep being herded along Cross Lane towards Sherlock's Abattoir on West High Street. Ironically passing the butcher's shop on the corner.

The land behind the Carlton also used to be home to travelling fairs. Many years ago, the stall holder of the rifle range was accidentally shot, and subsequently died of his wounds. The culprit was never caught.

Also at the back of the Carlton were their fire doors. If these were not closed properly, we would sneak into the cinema and watch films, such as Lawrence of Arabia, starring Peter O'Toole, or The Longest Day, with stars such as John Wayne, Henry Fonda, and Robert Mitchum.

Sundays were a special day. The day would start with us being awoken by The Salvation Army singing in the street. However, this did not please everybody, as some people wanted a lie in after a Saturday night on the ale.

Later in the morning my uncle Jim would visit. Uncle Jim was my father's brother. He would always bring a smile to my face with his jovial manner. My father and Jim would sit for a while talking, then they would be off to watch a Salford Sunday League football match. There were numerous games to choose from, as the league had six divisions with a total of seventy-two teams.

After watching a game, they would then go to Church. Well, that is what I thought, as it was in fact The Church Inn, one of the seventeen pubs on the half mile long, Cross Lane. The Church Inn was once a grocer's shop, which doubled in size when it took over the shop next door and extended to the rear. Although, to me, it seemed quite small, it was spotlessly clean. I remember the smell of pickled eggs, which were always on the bar.

After a few pints uncle Jim would go home, and my father would have a short sleep.

Next it would be our weekly visit to my auntie Peggy's. Peggy lived with her brother Albert in Myrtle Terrace, next to Cross Lane Railway Station.

We would have our tea there, which always consisted of tinned salmon sandwiches followed by tinned pineapple chunks covered in Carnation evaporated milk.

Uncle Albert liked to sing in the local pubs. Whilst we were there, he would be getting ready to go out, singing as he did so. One of his favourite pubs was The London and North-Western Hotel, better known as The Nor' West.

The Nor' West was once said to have one of the best concert halls in Lancashire.

Upon leaving auntie Peggy's, she would always give me sixpence. So, on the way home a visit to the sweet shop was our first call. What to buy was a hard choice, there were Spangles, 'Double wrapped to keep in the flavour' or Opal Fruits, 'Made to make your mouth water'. There were also Waggon Wheels, Jublies or a bottle of mineral. But my choice was usually my favourite, a Mars Bar at 6d which 'Helps you work, rest and play'.

Across the road from Auntie Peggy's was Sivori's Milk Bar, where all the latest machines were used. There was a soda fountain and an espresso coffee machine, serving frothy coffee in glass cups and saucers. This is where I had my first drink of hot Vimto. Also, on the high streets at this time, were cigarette machines and milk machines. To help you cross the road there was the new street furniture of push-button controlled Panda crossings.

Other food you could purchase on Cross Lane was hot potatoes from Lucetti's mobile oven, or black pudding and pig's feet from a woman pushing a pram. You could also be entertained by street musicians and travelling gypsy bands.

Myrtle Terrace, home of Aunty Peggy. Cross Lane Railway Station is on the right.

As October approached the world seemed to be on the brink of a nuclear war. Russia had sited nuclear missiles in Cuba, but after strong objections from America, the Soviet leader, Nikita Khrushchev backed down and removed the missiles.

The world could now relax and get back to normality. For me it meant preparing for bonfire night. The tradition of bonfire night dated back to November 5th, 1605. This was when a man named Guy Fawkes, and a group of plotters attempted to blow up the Houses of Parliament in London. They wanted to kill King James and his leaders. The reason for this assassination attempt started with the previous monarch, Queen Elizabeth 1st. She had made some laws against the Roman Catholics. Guy Fawkes and his friends thought these laws were unfair and hoped King James would change them. But in actual fact, the King enforced more laws against the Catholics.

So, a group of men led by Robert Catesby decided that the next time Parliament was opened by King James 1st, they would blow up everyone there with gunpowder. The men bought a house next door to the parliament building. The house had a cellar which went under the parliament building. They planned to place gunpowder under the house and then blow it up.

On 5th November, while keeping watch on the gunpowder, Guy Fawkes was discovered by the King's soldiers. In celebration of his survival, King James ordered the people of England to light great bonfires on the night of 5th November.

There was an unsubstantial story that the Gunpowder Plot was planned at Ordsal Hall, Salford.

A Guy would be made every year. In order to do this, old clothes were obtained and filled with newspaper, a balloon was used for the head and a mask finished the job off. The Guy could now be placed in an old pram or on the pavement. Outside shops would be a good place to site the Guy and ask people for 'A penny for the Guy'. But a better place would be the Carlton Casino, which had just replaced the cinema.

Another benefit of having the Carlton on our doorstep was, as the weather turned foggy, a peasouper, we could help people park their cars on the land behind the building.

The ideal time to do this was on a Saturday night when I was allowed to stay out later. This was for of two reasons. Firstly, there was no school the next day. Also Saturday was usually the day my parents would buy a new vinyl record to add to their collection. Usually a single, which cost 6/8d, or sometimes an LP, at 32/6d. They would then play through their collection, allowing me to stay out longer.

At this time, the Hit Parade had a number one named 'Telstar' by the Tornadoes. Whilst at number two was 'Let's dance' by Chris Montes. But more interesting was the record positioned at number 40. It was record performed on the clarinet by Acker Bilk, named 'Strangers on the Shore'. The record had been in the charts for over a year without reaching number one, although it did reach the number one position in America and stayed there for seven weeks. New to the charts was a group from Liverpool singing 'Love me Do'. The song was to reach number 17 in the charts, and the group was The Beatles.

In The News

August 5th, 1962. Actress Norma Jean Mortenson, better known as Marilyn Monroe, died of a drug overdose at the age of 36.

A selection of newspaper advertisements. You can see that the first one mentions Hylda Baker's new comedy film, taking its name from her famous catchphrase, 'She knows y' know'. Other's show the budget get-away deals, either by coach or ocean liner. A lot of families rented their television sets in the 1960's. The White's advert shows the weekly cost, but what stands out more is the size of the television, only 17 inches. Whereas today it is not uncommon to see 50-inch screens.

Top: A View across Salford Crescent. In the background stands to the left Salford Crescent Police Station. To the right is the Fire Station, with the Cenotaph directly in front. In the foreground stands the statue of Prince Albert, husband of Queen Victoria.

Bottom: Another view of Salford Crescent. This photograph was taken from Cross Lane roundabout. In the background can be seen The Salford University building. Before that is Windsor Bridge which passes over the railway line and canal. A scooter rider can be seen, together with two cyclists heading towards Cross Lane.

Views of Cross Lane in 1955

Top: Looking down Cross Lane from Broad Street. Note that the double decker bus in the foreground does not have a door at the back, passengers simply hopped on and off. To the left stands the Oliver Heywood obelisk, centred on an immaculate lawn.

Bottom: Looking back in the opposite direction. The single storey building on the left was one of many British Restaurants built to help the war effort. The larger building is the Cattle Market Hotel, one of many pubs on the Lane. In the background can be seen the market clock, further back is the chimney of the Salford Paint and Varnish Company.

Views of Salford in the 1930's

Top:- Trinity Market, better known as The Flat Iron Market. Earning its name because the area of land it stood on resembled the shape of a flat iron. In the foreground are bicycles left standing against the edging, all unlocked. In the background is the railway bridge crossing over Blackfriars Road.

FLAT IRON MARKET, 1933.

Cross Lane Cattle Market. The market was once one of the largest of its kind in England. Within its grounds there were six slaughterhouses and a bank, which can be seen to the right of the photograph. Note the ornate clock tower of the bank.

Another picture of Cross Lane Cattle Market

Chapter 6

<u>Winter</u>

Winter was fast approaching, and what a winter was in store for us.

As early as the second week in November snow blizzards covered the whole of Britain. Freezing fog followed, causing airports to close, with visibility down to as little as forty yards.

Smoke from the coal fires began to mix with the sulphur dioxide and turned into smog. The sulphur dioxide was created during the combustion of solid fuel. This was mainly in the houses of our area, but also from the steam trains passing nearby. Smog had not been seen on this scale since the Great Smog of 1952, when over ten thousand people died prematurely. There have since been measures introduced to eradicate this problem. In 1956 The Clean Air Act was introduced in order to reduce the air pollution. Some areas could only use smokeless fuel, and chimney heights were increased. Because of these terrible conditions there were many car crashes, with more than the average amount of lives being lost.

After a period of average weather came the start of 'The Big Freeze'. On the 22$^{nd\ of}$ December snow fell over the whole of Britain. In Salford there were six inches of snow on the ground, and twenty-five-foot snowdrifts were reported in some areas.

January saw no let-up in the freezing conditions, with nothing thawing out, the ice set in.

The cold-water pipe in our outside toilet was constantly freezing up. My father tried to remedy this by wrapping the pipe with old rags, but this proved ineffective.

His next attempt was to place a small oil lamp adjacent to the pipe, thus solving the problem.

Further disruption was caused when telephone cables were brought down by the weight of the snow and ice.

People were becoming stranded in their motor vehicles, some having to stay in their car overnight. This was also the case in small villages, where people could not venture from their homes. Troops were called in to assist in the clearing of the snowdrifts.

There was now a shortage of coal, which led to power cuts. Although our family was never short of coal, my dad had stockpiled it in readiness. Emergency water supplies were also required.

Farmers were now finding it particularly hard to manage. Livestock perished, milk could not be delivered, and hundreds of pounds worth of sugar beet and celery were lost to the Arctic conditions.

The hardships of the winter were lost to me and my friends. We loved the sight of snow on the ground and would play for hours throwing snowballs and making snowmen. We would build a sledge and carry it to Peel Park, where the hills were ideal for sledging.

However, the conditions were not ideal for my parents. Their nightly visit to the pub was now a hazardous journey, especially returning after a few pints of beer.

Deep snow at Humphrey Booth Gardens, Salford.
Note the ice forming to left of the building from a broken downpipe.

They now only visited the closest pubs such as The Wilton Arms, and The Buck Hotel. I would always wait up for their return and have a taste of the Milk Stout they would bring with them. Once they started talking about the pubs they had visited I could stay up for much longer.

One memorable story related to The Buck Hotel. Back in 1888, when the pub was ran by Mr and Mrs Twist, a famous customer visited. His name was Colonel WF Cody, better known as Buffalo Bill. He was in the area to perform his Wild West Show, a spectacular event featuring cowboys and Red Indians. This was held at the old Salford Racecourse, now the home of Salford Quays.

After the last of these shows Colonel Cody decided to have a few drinks before leaving for home. He later got a taxi to his Howard Street lodging house. On arriving home an argument erupted regarding the route taken by the taxi driver. Thus, Mr Cody refused to pay the fare and eventually came to blows with the driver. The next day a summons was issued for Mr Cody to appear before a Salford Court.

However, Mr Cody was busy preparing his return to America, and so pleaded guilty to assault in his absence. He received a three pound fine, plus costs. His representative paid the fine for him.

Unable to coax more stories from my parents, it was now time for bed. Although the bedrooms were cold, mine was directly over the living room, therefore benefiting from some of the residual heat. Whereas my parents' bedroom was freezing and a place I rarely visited in winter. They would always place a hot water bottle in bed and a two-bar electric fire would just about stop ice forming on the windows.

The next day it was school as usual, I was quite content to take the journey hardly wrapped up, in fact I would even wear short trousers. This was not the case for my mother, she would wear a large coat, woolly hat, scarf, thick socks, and Wellington boots, with the thickest of long trousers tucked inside them. It was now a common sight to see bottles of milk on doorsteps freezing up, and the frozen milk protruding from the top of the bottle.

The weather conditions continued to deteriorate, freezing fog and drizzle caused black ice to form on many roads, resulting in many road accidents.

Thousands of tons of salt had been used for the gritting of roads, so supplies were now at an all-time low.

More recently, a Heron stands on my garden pond cover. But the fish underneath it are safe.

Many rivers had become frozen, and this now began to stretch out to the sea. Ice flows could be seen off many coastlines. A common sight under Windsor Bridge would be children ice skating on the frozen cut canal, oblivious to any danger.

As temperatures dropped, diesel fuel in buses and lorries froze. Water and gas mains also fell victim to the extremely cold weather. Locally, in Salford there was a tragedy when a gas main fractured, resulting in gas escaping which caused the death of five people through poisoning

Salting the roads was becoming ineffective, as even the salt water froze. British Rail cancelled many train journeys because of the ice forming on the train tracks, and trains freezing up whilst still in motion.

During the month of January, the temperatures plummeted to their lowest of the winter. Many people could not reach their place of work, and some jobs proved impossible to do, especially in the building trade. That was with the exception of plumbers, who were in great demand for repairing burst pipes.

The severe weather conditions saw the introduction of the Football Pools Panel. This was a panel of five people who would predict the outcome of abandoned football matches. These predictions were only for the sake of the football coupon and did not affect the team's positions in the league. The first of these panels sat on January 26th. It consisted of four former professional footballers, Ted Drake, Tommy Lawton, Tom Finney, and George Young. The other member of the panel being ex referee, Arthur Ellis. Chairman of the panel was former Tory MP, John Theodore Cuthbert Moore-Brabazon, 1st Baron Brabazon of Tara.

For the first time in nearly fifty years frozen conger eels were washed ashore on the East coast. Wildlife was a continual problem affecting the food chain. Birds were eating vegetables before they could be harvested. Root crops, intended for livestock were being eaten by hungry wild animals. Throughout January it was recorded that temperatures never rose above zero degrees Celsius. Thus, it went down in history as the coldest month of this century. When February arrived so did more snow and fog. Snowdrifts caused most of the roads in Southwest to be closed. By the end of the month there were signs of a thaw. Although this would bring problems of its own, with major flooding occurring in the South of England.

However, this was no thaw in Scotland, which was now experiencing their worst snowfalls of the winter.

This winter had now become officially the coldest since 1740.

It wasn't until the end of first week in March that the temperature began to rise. The sun was out, and at last, winter was a thing of the past.

As the thaw set in, swans on the canal could now swim in between the blocks of ice.

In the News.

January 1963. Hugh Gaitskell, leader of the Labour Party, died suddenly. Harold Wilson stepped into the position.

Chapter 7

Spring 1963

It was a relief to see the end of that terrible winter, although we now entered a period of great uncertainty.

This was because a government committee, led by Doctor Richard Beeching was looking into more cost-effective ways of running Britain's Railways. The resulting report recommended that over two thousand railway stations should close, thus cutting off many rail links to outlying areas.

This news brought great concern to our area, as the majority of families relied on the railway companies for their livelihood.

But for now, we would have to wait and see what the final outcome would be, as the report would not go before Parliament until later this year.

Back at school, it was time for the annual medical inspection. This would start with the nit nurse rummaging through your hair in search for any of the horrible tiny creatures. Nits were a lot more common in this era, as hair washing was not a daily routine.

Next it would be the inoculations against the diseases Polio, Diphtheria, and Tuberculosis. This meant that a vaccine would be introduced into your body in order to produce immunity against the diseases.

Unfortunately, the vaccine would be administered by a large needle, to my great dismay.

The final examination would be a dental check. If any problems were encountered, it would mean a visit to the dentist at Regent Road Clinic.

I do remember being quite at ease on my first visit there, as I had never been before. This was soon to change.

After a quick examination the dentist said I needed a filling and three teeth extracting. The filling would be done immediately. He then proceeded to produce a syringe in order to administer cocaine into my gums, so that I would feel no pain. But, as I was about to find out, this would not be a 100% effective pain reliever.

The teeth would have to be extracted at another dental practice. There you would be sedated with a gas called nitrous oxide, commonly called laughing gas. I don't know if the gas was meant to put you completely asleep, but I certainly remember having some strange dreams during the procedure.

Subsequent visits to the dentist would fill me with great terror.

After these two hiccups to the start of 1963, I could now look forward to the rest of the year. For this would be a year I would remember above most others.

Saturday was my favourite day of the week. It would begin with a visit to the children's club at the Carlton Cinema. The Cinema would be full of children, with only a handful of adults to supervise them.

After a short musical introduction, the manager would host some birthday singing and talent shows. But it was the films that most children had come to see.

Films such as King Kong, and Flash Gordon were favourites. Enjoyed even more while enjoying a tub of vanilla ice cream, eaten with the obligatory wooden spoon.

The number five single decker bus, which would take us into town.
Seen here leaving Victoria Bus Station.

After the Children's Club my mother would sometimes take me into Town. We would catch the number three or number five bus from Liverpool Street to Victoria Bus Station.

We would then walk the short distance into Manchester town centre. Wile's toy shop was a favourite port of call. Amongst other things, there were the Hornby train set layouts, and Airfix modelling kits to admire.

My mother would always include a visit to the United Cattle Products shop, better known as the UCP. She would buy pig's feet and a tray of faggots. I was never keen on any of the products from this shop.

A more interesting shop was Barry's Record Rendezvous. This shop was packed with shelves full of vinyl records, old and new. There were many new groups coming onto the music scene, such as The Beatles, The

Rolling Stones, Herman's Hermits, Gerry and the Pacemakers, and local group, The Hollies. Many of these groups performed at The Cavern Club in Liverpool, joined by up-and-coming bands such as The Swinging Blue Jeans, The Remo Four, and The Four Jays, later renamed The Fourmost.

Unfortunately, these groups were not on my parents radar. It would be more likely they would choose a Nat King Cole record. A recording artist I would appreciate more as I got older.

A new building worth a visit was the CIS. When built, in 1962, it was the third tallest building in Europe. Only overshadowed by The Pirelli Building in Milan, and Madrid's Torre De Madrid. On the roof of the CIS, if the weather permitted, you could see the Clywidian Mountains in Wales. On returning home, and if a haircut was required, it usually took place on a Saturday. There were two local barbers to choose from. On Liverpool Street was Charlie's, and for 9d you could get a short back and sides. But for 1/3d, Eric Staton on Cross Lane would do you a square neck, the latest vogue in hair styling. Eric's barber shop was the more modern type, sometimes referred to as a hairdressing salon. He had framed, and signed drawings of some of his more famous customers hung on the wall. Whilst in Charlie's shop there would be no such modern décor and just the one choice of haircut, which was one step up from a basin cut. But because it was 6d cheaper I would normally end up having to go to Charlie's, unless I could afford to pay the difference out of my 2/- a week spends.

The junction of Cross Lane and Liverpool Street. Behind the man crossing the road is Sewell's Hardware Shop, with bus stop adjacent, which sat directly opposite Charlie's Barber Shop.

The remainder of Saturday afternoon was usually taken up with a game of football.

This Saturday routine would continue until one afternoon in May, when my life would be transformed for ever.

The day was May 25th, 1963. We had put our jumpers down as goalposts and were enjoying a game of football. Although on this particular day the game was constantly interrupted by the sound of steam trains passing by. The game would stop whilst we looked at the trains, and to our surprise the trains were uncommon to the area.

I decided to go home and ask my dad about the unusual phenomenon.

My dad's face was a picture, it seemed he could not wait to tell me the reason.

'Well son, the vast number of trains are necessary to transport football fans to The FA Cup Final. Furthermore, the final will be contested between Manchester United and Leicester City. Therefore, the trains are needed to take United fans to Wembley.'

My dad had been a United fan for many years and spoke with great pride about the team. He decided to watch the game on television at my Grandad's house and would take me with him.

So, it was Shank's Pony to Grandad's house, which was at the bottom end of Regent Road. Although it was quite a long walk, the trek was interrupted by stopping at the toffee shop. There we bought Pontefract Cakes, a bottle of mineral, a bag of Kali, and Spanish to dip in it.

On arriving at Grandad's my dad said he would give me threepence each for every goal United scored. This seemed a great surprise to Grandad, as he was not used to such extravagance.

The possibility of a few goals being scored was quite high. All British football teams in the sixties played using a 2-3-5 formation. This was two full backs, three half backs, and five strikers.

That was not the only difference in the way football was set up compared with today. All League and FA Cup matches were played on a Saturday afternoon, kick off at 3pm. This was from August until the end of April. The FA Cup Final would then be played on the first Saturday in May. This year would be an exception because of the vast number of games postponed during the winter.

On the long walk to Grandad's house, we passed many shops and pubs.
This photograph shows The Wheatsheaf Pub on the corner of West Albion Street.
Note the ladies looking in the shop window, all wearing head scarves.

The only matches shown on television were The FA Cup Final and International matches. Midweek was reserved for European games, and FA Cup replays. There were no games on a Sunday.

The FA Cup replays would carry on until there was a winner, without the aid of a penalty shoot-out.

The football stadiums of this era mostly catered for people who would be standing to watch the match, which created a great atmosphere. There were no all seater stadiums in Britain.

The seating areas were usually reserved for season ticket holders, of which there were very few. The remainder of the fans would pay at the turnstile.

Many fans would go to a match adorned with a rosette, bar scarf, and carrying a wooden rattle, whose noise would add to the atmosphere. There were no replica football shirts available.

The shirts the players wore did not have their names on the back. But simply a number from 1 to 11, no squad numbers in those days, and sponsors did not exist. It was only in the FA Cup Final that the team badge appeared on the shirt.

There were however, improvements with the football equipment. There was the introduction of lightweight football boots, progressing from the rugby type boots with ankle protectors. The new screw in studs allowed players to easily change them for different playing conditions. Even the footballs were made more waterproof, not getting very heavy when wet.

Surely with all these improvements United would score a bagful of goals.

The corner of Cross Lane and Liverpool Street. Fred Oddie's Butcher shop is on the corner. Next door is Davis's newsagent, then The Buck Hotel.

In The News

On March 24th the Alcatraz Federal Penitentiary, built on Alcatraz Island in San Francisco Bay, closed. The last 27 prisoners were transferred to other jails on the order of The United States Attorney General, Robert F Kennedy.

Chapter 8

The 1963 FA Cup Final

This was the centenary year for the Football Association and the Cup Final would be contested by Manchester United and Leicester City. One hundred thousand tickets were sold, bringing in record gate receipts of £89,000.

For United this was the culmination of five years of rebuilding after the tragic Munich air disaster which happened on the 6th of February 1958. In the accident twenty-three people lost their lives, including eight players. Also, manager Matt Busby was so badly injured that he did not resume full-time work until 1960.

Leicester City were clear favourites to win the final. They had finished fourth in division one on their previous campaign, whereas United could only manage nineteenth place. Although only having two full international players, in Banks and Gibson, City were quite a talented outfit.

After losing to Tottenham Hotspur in 1961 they had strengthened their team. In came strikers Davie Gibson and Mike Stringfellow, they cost £25,000 each and arrived in the same week of 1962. Having also lost to Wolves in the 1949 final they were hoping this would be third time lucky.

The United team however, was packed with international players, but unlike Leicester they had failed to gel in their league campaign. It was a different matter in the cup, where they seemed to play their best football.

In the third round they were drawn to play Huddersfield Town from the second division. In front of 47,703 Old Trafford fans, they came out comfortable winners 5-0. Denis law scored a hat trick, Johnny Giles and Albert Quixall getting the others.

The fourth round saw United at home again, this time against first division Aston Villa. 52,265 people saw Albert Quixall get the only goal of the game, seeing United safely through to the fifth round.

Again, United were drawn at home, this time to a Chelsea side riding high in the second division. But facing United proved a bridge too far for Chelsea, they were dispatched 2-1, goals coming from Denis Law and Albert Quixall to the delight of most of the 48,298 fans.

There would be no more home games for United in this campaign. For in the quarter final, they were drawn away against third division Coventry City. A Highfield Road crowd of 44,000 witnessed a pulsating game with United running out 3-1 winners thanks to two goals from Bobby Charlton and one from that man again, Albert Quixall.

Villa Park was picked as the venue for the semi-final. Second division Southampton were United's opponents, and 65,000 fans watched an enthralling game with United reaching the FA Cup Final thanks to the only goal of the game being scored by Denis Law.

It would now be an agonising decision for Matt Busby to decide on the line up for the final. Although playing many games of the previous season, Harry Gregg, Shay Brennan, and Nobby Stiles would be omitted. The following team would line up for the final.

Dave Gaskell

Twenty-two-year-old David has been at United since 1955. Born in Wigan, he made his goalkeeping debut for the first team at the age of sixteen in the 1956 Charity Shield against Manchester City.

Tony Dunne

Dublin-born right back Patrick Anthony Dunne joined United from Irish club, Shelbourne in 1960. He got his chance that season when Shay Brennan was injured and had never looked back. A very fast, tough defender, twenty-one-year-old Tony looked to have a great future ahead of him.

Noel Cantwell

Captain for the day was this elegant Republic of Ireland international left back. Noel was signed from West Ham United in 1960 for £29,500. His leadership qualities led the manager to install the thirty-year old as team captain in place of Maurice Setters.

Pat Crerand

Signed from Glasgow Celtic for a reported fee of £43,000 in the February of 1963, twenty-four-years old, right half Paddy is United's latest recruit. Although he never wanted to move from Celtic, when United offered to double his wages to £45 a week, plus bonuses, he decided to move over the border.

Bill Foulkes

At centre half Bill was the veteran of the team, and their longest serving player, being at the club since 1950. Then 31, he started his career as a full back, and it was at this position he gained his only England cap, against Northern Ireland in 1954. A survivor of the Munich disaster, he was later converted to centre half.

Maurice Setters

Former captain Maurice would occupy the number six shirt. This twenty-six-year-old joined United from West Bromwich Albion in 1960 for a fee of £30,000. A robust, tough tackling wing half, he added the steel to Pat Crerand's finesse.

Albert Quixall

In 1958 Sheffield Wednesday sold their wing wizard, Albert, to United for £45,000. At the time this was a European record transfer fee. Having gained experience playing for England alongside Stanley Matthews, could this twenty-nine-year-old take centre stage?

Johnny Giles

The third Republic of Ireland international in the team, Johnny has been at United since 1956. This twenty-two-year-old was spotted playing for Irish league club Home Farm, and on that day, he would play in his least favourite position at outside right.

David Herd

On joining United from Arsenal in July 1961, Dave, then twenty-nine, had a reputation as a prolific goal scorer. Which he proved in his first season, scoring in one out of every two games. Thus, proving his £35,000 fee justified. Born in Scotland, he once played in the same Stockport County team as his father, Alex.

Denis Law

A British record transfer fee of £115,000 was paid to Torino for Denis in 1962. Matt Busby had tried, unsuccessfully, to sign him as a sixteen-year-old, and also had given him his Scotland debut at the age of eighteen. Now twenty-three, this striker was the jewel in United's crown.

Bobby Charlton

Another Munich disaster survivor, Bobby joined United from junior football in 1953. Then twenty-five, he also had a brother, Jackie, who played for Leeds United. Bobby soon gained a reputation for his thunderbolt shot and was given his first team debut in 1956 against, aptly named Charlton Athletic. Although he scored twice, he was dropped for the next game to make way for Tommy Taylor. But he soon became an integral part of the great 'Busby Babes', he would go on to score ten goals in sixteen games in the 1956/57 season. After the Munich disaster it was a great comfort to Matt Busby that Bobby was there to inspire the rest of the team.

It was on the afternoon of the 25th of May 1963 Manchester United were led out at Wembley Stadium by manager Matt Busby. After the National Anthem was played, captain Noel Cantwell introduced his players to His Royal Highness, The Prince Philip, after which the players broke for a warmup.

For the sake of the television coverage one of the teams would have to change their kit. As United won the toss it would be City who would play in all white, United would play in their usual red and white colours. It was United to kick off the final and for the first ten minutes the teams were evenly matched. After this initial period United took control of the game and bombarded the Leicester City goal. United were so quick to the ball that Leicester were finding it difficult to get out of their own half. The middle of the park was completely dominated by the Scottish duo of Law and Crerand.

It appeared that Denis Law wanted to cover as much of that famous Wembley turf as he could. The ball was quickly being distributed through the middle to Herd and Quixall, and out on the wings to Charlton and Giles. In defence, Foulkes, Cantwell and Dunne were faultless. With the added assistance of Setters and Crerand, City were finding it difficult to get a shot on goal.

Undoubtedly the busiest player on the pitch was Gordon Banks in the Leicester City goal. Shots were on target from United strikers Charlton, Herd and Quixall. Wing halves Crerand and Setters also got in on the act, bringing saves from Banks.

Matt Busby had bought Paddy Crerand mainly because he thought he would be the ideal link from midfield to provide the ball to Denis Law. In the 30th minute this is exactly what he did. Paddy intercepted a poor throw out from Gordon Banks about thirty yards from goal and took it forward into the City penalty area, he squared the ball across the box to Denis. In a split second he spun around, and the ball was in the net 1-0.

United continued to dominate the game, Charlton and Law both coming close to increasing their lead. Notably, Crerand seemed to be growing in stature as the game went on.

He had completely nullified City's play maker, Davie Gibson, restricting City to a solitary goal attempt, whilst United had over a dozen. Leicester City manager Matt Gillies must have been the happiest man in the stadium when half time arrived. For now, the onslaught was halted, and he could regroup his players, who were extremely lucky to be only one goal behind.

They kicked off the second half and were immediately showing more purpose. In the 53rd minute a high ball was hit into United's penalty area by Riley and was handled nervously by Gaskell, allowing the ball to slip from his grasp, but City could not capitalise on this mistake and four minutes later it was United who increased their lead.

Crerand received the ball on the edge of his penalty area, he fed the ball through to Giles, who threaded it towards the left of the pitch. A fast-advancing Charlton collected the ball without breaking stride before unleashing one of his trademark thunderbolt shots at the Leicester goal. Banks could not hold on to the ball and parried it nicely for Herd to put the ball in the net 2-0.

Front and back covers of the 1963 FA Cup Final programme.
These were the only two pages in the programme containing any colour.

Now with a two-goal advantage, United slowed the tempo down. Still having the majority of the play, they were not allowing Leicester any substantial goal attempts.

The game had flowed, without any interruptions until the 76th minute. Now for the first time we saw team trainer Jack Crompton come on to treat the injured Herd.

But within four minutes the unthinkable happened, Leicester scored. McKlintock tried a shot from thirty yards out which hit a United player and rebounded straight back to him. He tried another shot which seemed to be going wide of the goal. But there was Keyworth to get his head to the ball and send it into the corner of United's net 2-1.

We now saw more urgency in United's play, they wanted to finish off a revitalised Leicester side. A high ball hit into the Leicester penalty area was met perfectly by Law, but the ball glanced off the goal post.

In the 85th minute Crerand received the ball just inside his own half, he glided past two players before releasing an inch perfect pass to Giles on the right. He moved forward a few yards and floated the ball into the Leicester penalty area. Once again, the ball was fumbled by Banks and there was the grateful Herd to put the ball in the net 3-1.

That goal would see the end of Leicester's brief revival, Manchester United, were deservedly the 1963 FA Cup winners. Thus, helping to erase memories of the defeats in the 1957 and 1958 Finals.   Although this was a great team effort, two players stood out. It was evident that only the groundsman had covered more blades of grass than Denis Law. But undoubtedly the man of the match was Paddy Crerand, who was reminiscent of an orchestra leader, conducting the players of his team with great panache.

Captain, Noel Cantwell climbed the Wembley steps to collect the cup from Her Majesty Queen Elizabeth 2nd. This triumph has been the culmination of a massive rebuilding plan. Lots of hard work by manager Matt Busby, ably assisted by his assistant, Jimmy Murphy, had finally come to fruition.

In The News

Jim Clark, born 4th March 1936, became the youngest ever Formula One Grand Prix winner. Driving the Lotus25, he won seven out of the ten races.

Top: Action from the Cup Final. Tony Dunne, closest to the ball and other players look on anxiously as the ball runs out of play.

Bottom: From left to right the United players, Gaskell, Dunne, Charlton, Cantwell, Crerand, Quixall, and Herd, celebrate with the FA Cup. It looks like Bobby is a bit parched, taking in some water from a wet sponge.

Above: The Manchester United FA Cup squad. From left to right, Trainer Jack Crompton, Brennan, Setters, Gregg, Gaskell, Foulkes, Herd, Charlton, Dunne, Giles, Quixall, Cantwell Law, Crerand, Stiles.

Below: What the average football fan would take to the final: - Wooden rattle, scarf, bobble hat, and rosette.

Chapter 9

Football Crazy

 I recall collecting the ninepence treat off my dad and thinking to myself this is money for old rope. If I could collect threpence for every goal United scored, I would soon have enough money to go and watch them play live.

Unfortunately, it was a one-off treat for the televised FA Cup Final. I had however, now caught the football bug, and would take every opportunity to play the game. At school I would play football in the playground at every break from lessons. Once I got home from school, it was a quick change of clothes and straight out to play football. If there were none of my friends out, I would make do with kicking the ball against a brick wall. It only needed another player, and we could have a game of wally, each of us only having one kick of the ball to hit the wall. But once all my mates came out, we would put our jumpers down as goalposts and have a full-scale game on the croft behind the Carlton Cinema.

Football aside we must not forget that this was now the cricket season. So, we would still chalk the wickets on the wall and play the game.

It was only the previous month that we had visited Old Trafford, which is Lancashire County's cricket ground. There we watched the first one-day county cricket match, in which Lancashire beat Leicestershire. Ironically the match went into the second day because of bad weather.

The match was actually a preliminary knock-out game to decide which team would fill the 16th place in a new one-day cup competition.

The competition, sponsored by an American razor company would be called the Gillette Cup.

A month after this game Old Trafford would bear witness one of the greatest test teams of all time. The West Indies arrived for the first test of five against England.

Their team was packed full of talent and was captained by the legendary Frank Worrell. Their line up included batsmen such as Rohan Kanhai, Conrad Hunte, Basil Butcher, and the all-rounder Gary Sobers. To add to the bowling of Sobers they also had the spinner Lance Gibbs, and the pace men Charlie Griffiths and Wes Hall.

 England also had a decent team, with the likes of Colin Cowdrey, Ted Dexter, Ken Barrington, Fred Truman, and Brian Statham. But they were no match for the West Indies, who scored 501 runs for six wickets declared. This was mainly due to Conrad Hunte scoring 182 runs. England scored 205 runs in their first innings and were forced to follow on. But their second innings score of 296 meant they finished on level scores. So, the West Indies came out to get the one run required.

It was not long before the school summer holidays were upon us. Several weeks off school, which was great for children, but a nightmare for parents. They would have to put up with their mithering children all day long.

However, my dad would alleviate the burden for my mam by taking me to his workplace with him. We would catch the number 70 bus, which would take us along Trafford Road, and we would get off on the Salford side of Trafford swing bridge. A brisk walk across the bridge to Trafford Park Road and the iconic Liverpool Warehousing Co. In front of the warehouse there were railway tracks, which were used to transport goods to various locations.

One hundred yards on and we turned onto Warwick Road, and there it was, the now named, 'Theatre of Dreams', Manchester United's football stadium. We made our way down the side of the ground, around the back of Glovers Cable factory and arrived at the railway sheds where my dad worked.

We had a quick brew, the tea brewed in a metal enamelled brew-can whose top was the cup. It was now time to do some work, well it was for my dad. He loaded the steam train with coal and soon it was ready to leave the sheds. I was allowed on the footplate of the train and to throw a few pieces of coal on the roaring fire, which was needed to power the train.

After finishing my day's work, I would make my way home, but not without paying a visit to Old Trafford football ground. The players were now back in training, and I could take this opportunity to collect some autographs.

As soon as a player got out of his car he was engulfed by an army of autograph hunters. It was not always possible to collect the autographs of all the players, so I would wait until the training session had finished and get the one's I had missed.

Whilst waiting, there were a few youth team players having a kick about outside the ground. One particular player stood out above the rest, so I decided to ask him for his autograph, 'no problem' said George Best.

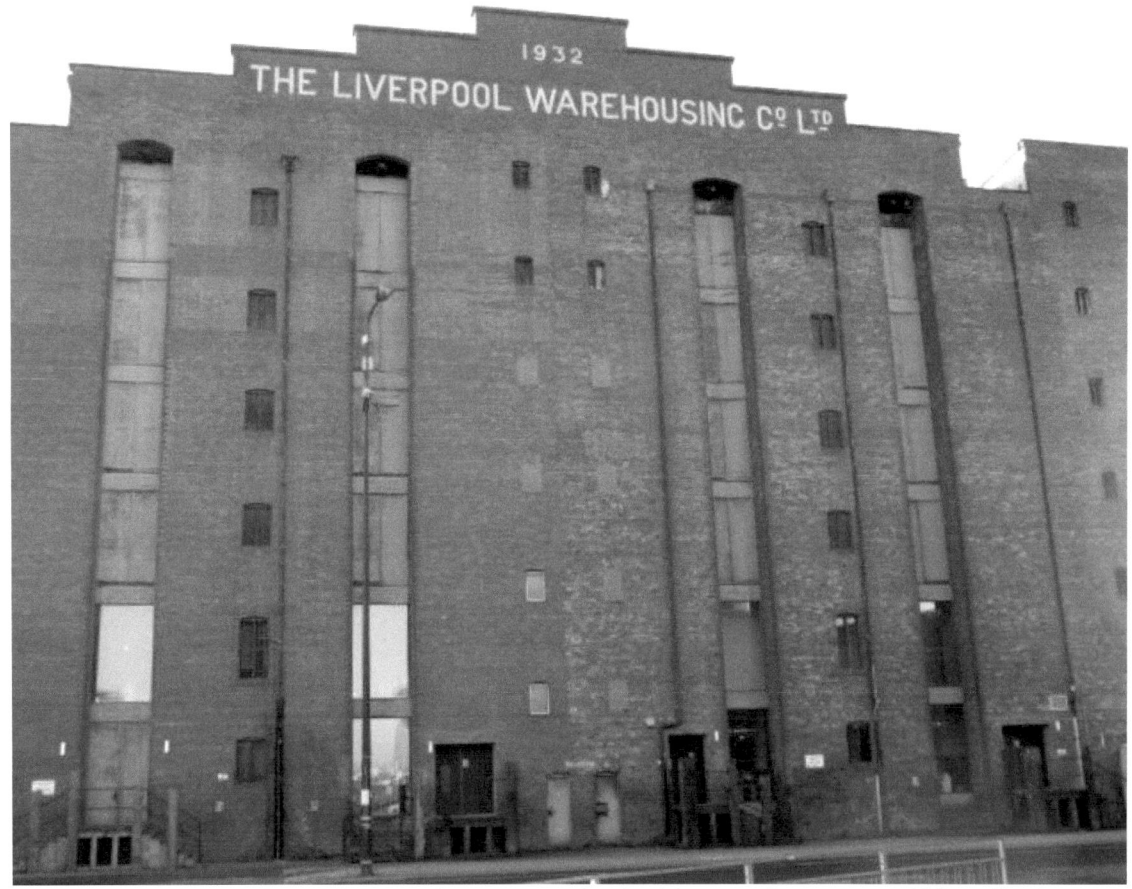
Many a football fan will remember passing this building on their way to Old Trafford. Situated only a few hundred yards from the ground, it was once used for the storage and distribution of cotton.

On August 8th came the news of an incredible heist. This took place in Buckinghamshire and involved the robbery of a Post Office train travelling from Glasgow to London.

A gang of criminals stopped the train and stole 120 sacks of money containing approximately £2.5 million. The raid, carried out with military precision, became known as 'The Great Train Robbery'.

Nearer to home, the Carlton Cinema underwent a major transformation. After a great deal of refurbishment, it reopened as the Carlton Casino. It had a cinema upstairs, and a casino downstairs. The cinema admission for the opening night was 2d.

This coincided with the start of the new football season, which for me was somewhat an anti-climax, as United lost 0-4 to Everton in the Charity Shield.

So, for the first league game Matt Busby decided to make a few team changes. One of the players left out of the team was Johnny Giles. Already unhappy at being played out of his favourite position, Johnny put in a transfer request. He subsequently joined Leeds United, but a lot of United fans were sorry to see him leave.

But United persevered without him and made a promising start to the new campaign. After gaining revenge over Everton with a 5-1 win, United found themselves top of the league.

For me there would be four landmark games in 1963. The first was the FA Cup Final, and the second was just about to happen.

On September 14th United gave a debut to the young apprentice I had watched having a kick about outside Old Trafford. Seventeen-year-old George Best was included in the team to play West Bromwich Albion and impressed in the 1-0 win.

But these two games were insignificant compared to the third game in my landmark quartet. This was the first division clash with West Ham United on 26th October.

The weekend started off as usual on the day before this match. After finishing school on the Friday, I paid my weekly visit to Hodge Lane wash baths. We now used the wash baths instead of going through the rigmarole of setting up and filling the tin bath.

This was better for everyone, and we even did not have to clean the bath afterwards, as it was all done for you.

After the wash baths it was Friday night chippy. We would call at Greasy Emma's fish and chip shop for our tea. It would normally be pudding and chips all round, the puddings being carried home in a pot basin.

When our meal was over my dad came out with a bombshell, ' Would you like to come with me tomorrow to watch Manchester United play West Ham United?'

Well, you could have knocked me down with a feather. 'Yes please,' I replied, not being able to contain my excitement.

My immediate thought was to run down to the swap shop and see if the wooden football rattle was still in the window. The swap shop had opened earlier in the year, selling, or swapping second hand goods. So, I set my sights on doing a deal with the owner of the shop to obtain the rattle, as soon as the shop opened the next day.

Because of the excitement I hardly slept that night and was up at the crack of dawn. I gathered together a platoon of my plastic soldiers and headed down to the swap shop. The trade was too good for the owner to turn down, and the rattle was mine.

Now for people who are not familiar with the wooden rattle. It was spun around in your hand and made a very loud noise. This would be ideal at the match, but when I tried it at home my mam was not impressed. But she did give me a hand knitted woollen football scarf, she had secretly been making at home.

Now I was itching to get on my way to Old Trafford, but it was far too early for my dad. As it got to 1pm he finally gave in to my pestering. I gathered my scarf and rattle, and we set off down Cross Lane.

Our route to the match would take us past this busy junction
where Cross Lane carries on to Trafford Road

Our first stop was Sivori's Cafe, for my first taste of a hot Vimto cordial drink, before jumping on the bus. We took the same route as we did to my dad's workplace in the summer.

Only this time it was different, as we neared the ground, we could hear the fans singing, then when we turned onto Warwick Road the full crescendo hit us.

> *Oh, the lads, you should've seen us coming.*
> *The fastest team in the league, just to see us running.*
> *All the lads and lasses, with smiles upon their faces.*
> *Walking down the Warwick Road, to see Matt Busby's Aces*

Outside the ground there were large crowds of people milling around. There were stalls selling all kind of souvenirs, my dad bought me a rosette to go with my scarf and rattle.

We entered the ground at the United Road side and made our way to the front rail for a better view. This was the best place for children as stadiums were mostly all standing. Also, we could purchase refreshments from a white-coated vendor pushing his trolley around the perimeter of the pitch. Hot Bovril drink and crisps was my dad's recommendation.

By the time the kick off came along, 45,000 people were in the stadium. Not a full house, as West Ham United were in the bottom half of division one.

As the teams were announced, United had only three changes from the Cup Final team. Giles had left the club and was replaced by Chisnall. Gregg replaced Gaskell in goal, and Moir came in for Quixall. The West Ham team had some talented players in Bobby Moore, Geoff Hurst, and Martin Peters.

In a hard-fought game, West Ham came out the winners 1-0. Although United lost, the day had been a fantastic experience which would never be forgotten.

Bad news for horse racing fans was the closure of Manchester Racecourse. Situated at Castle Irwell, Salford, it had been the venue of some of the best horse races in the country. Races such as The November Handicap, and Lancashire Oaks had been held there. So, on 9th November, over 20,000 fans watched the last race, The Goodbye Consolation Plate. The winning jockey being Lester Piggott, on Fury Royal.

Leeds United manager, Don Revie walks away from Old Trafford with bargain buy, Johnny Giles.

On 22nd November news came out of the USA that shocked the world. Their President, John F Kennedy was assassinated. He was shot dead as he was driven through Dallas on his way to a political meeting. Lee Harvey Oswald was later charged with his murder.

On a lighter note, the next day we saw the first episode of a new series on our TV screen, it was called, Dr. Who.

Back to the football, and my fourth landmark game of the year was upon us. United played a newly promoted Stoke City team, which included 48-year-old Stanley Matthews. Best remembered for the so called 'Matthews Final'. This was the FA Cup Final of 1953, when he put in an outstanding display to help his club, at that time Blackpool, win the cup. However, this game belonged to Denis Law, who scored four goals in a 5-2 United win.

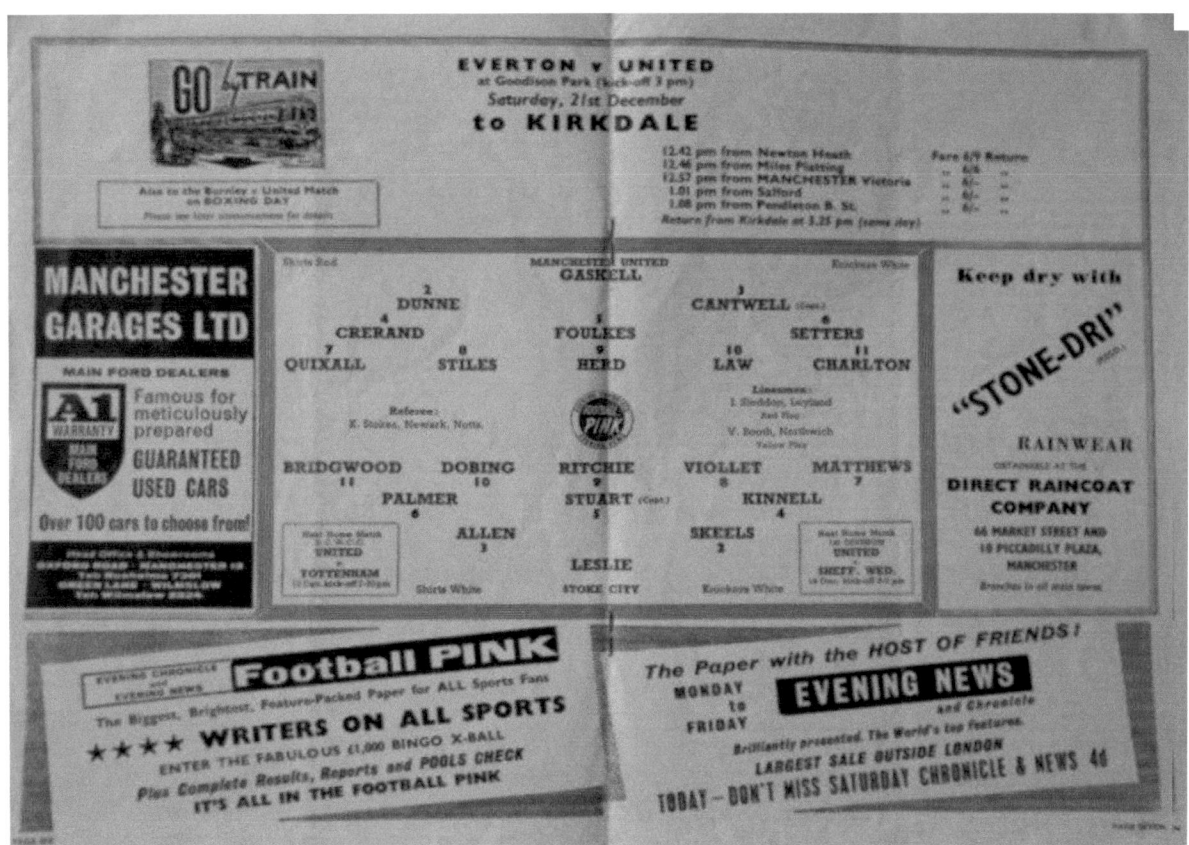
The team line ups for the match against Stoke City. Note ex United legend Denis Viollet at number eight.

Christmas time was on the horizon, and I now began to wonder to what presents I would receive. My mam took me to see Father Christmas at Lewis's apartment store in Manchester city centre.

The queues were so long that they carried on down the stairs and out onto the street. But whilst waiting we could buy some hot roasted chestnuts from a street vendor.

When we finally reached Father Christmas, I handed him a written note with the things I would like for Christmas. Top of the list was a racing bike, but at £25, it was maybe a bit optimistic. Other items on my list were a Monopoly Set, Action Man, Meccano Set, a box of Lego bricks, and a Train

Set.

On returning home my mother would begin to decorate the Christmas tree. The tree was artificial and quite small. The decorations consisted of tinsel, large baubles, chocolate coins wrapped in gold foil, and small pieces of cotton wool for the snow effect. We also had some ceiling decorations, which were coloured paper and could be folded up like a concertina, to be stored away.

On Christmas morning I was up at the crack of dawn, and at the bottom of the bed were my presents. The bike wasn't there, but I did get a Monopoly Set, box of Lego bricks, and a Train Set. I was happy with three out of six on my list.

A lot of the day and evening we would sit in front of the television, as the programmes were of a much better standard than normal. Christmas time would be the only time of the year that my parents would purchase the Radio Times and TV Times. In them would be the listings for all the television programs over the Christmas period.

On Christmas day our dinner would be followed by a Christmas pudding. My dad took great joy in pouring brandy over the pudding before setting it alight. A sixpence coin was concealed in the pudding, and whoever had it in their portion could keep it.

In the evening my parents would indulge themselves in their other Christmas treats. For my dad it would be a King Edward cigar, and a few bottles of Brown Ale. For my mother it would be a small bottle of Cherry B, followed by a few Babychams, although the bottles were very small.

After a few drinks she would come out with a little ditty:

Oh, you are a funny un.
Your face is like a pickled onion.
A nose like a squashed tomato,
and legs like match sticks

On Boxing Day, it seemed that most of the Football First Division teams were still full of the Christmas spirit.

There were ten games played and a total of sixty-six goals scored. The games were as follows:-

 Blackpool 1 - Chelsea 5
 Burnley 6 - Manchester United 1
 Fulham 10 - Ipswich 1
 Leicester City 2 - Everton 0
 Liverpool 6 - Stoke City 1
 Nottingham Forest 3 - Sheffield United 3
 Sheffield Wednesday 3 - Bolton Wanderers 0

West Bromwich Albion 4 - Tottenham Hotspur 4
West Ham United 2 - Blackburn Rovers 8
Wolverhampton Wanderers 3 - Aston Villa 3

Looking back at the events of 1963 we had witnessed the introduction of the Ford Cortina MK1, with a starting price of £910. Or you could go for the Hillman Imp, which was unique in that the engine was in the boot.

This year also saw the introduction of the compact tape cassette, and the Sindy Doll as a rival to the Barbie Doll.

But for myself, I had found a new passion in life, which was football.

In The News

Martin Luther King Junior delivers the 'I Have a Dream' speech on the steps of The Lincoln Memorial. There were said to be over 250,000 people in attendance.

Chapter 10

1964

On the first day of the New Year a new music program was introduced onto our television screens. Called 'Top of the Pops', it was produced in Studio A, on Dickenson Road, Rusholme, Manchester. It featured performances from the best-selling pop artists of the time, and soon became a Thursday night favourite.

The program was the second music show to hit our screens in the last five months. Already established on Friday nights was Ready Steady Go, with the popular catch phrase, 'The Weekend Starts Here'. It's theme tune was 5-4-3-2-1, sung by Manfred Mann.

Paul Jones of Manfred Man singing the song 5-4-3-2-1 on Ready Steady Go…

Not long after this the USA welcomed an invasion of the best of Britain's pop stars. Herman's Hermits were the most successful, followed by

The Dave Clark Five, The Animals, The Who, and of course The Beatles.

Back in Britain, The Beatles were now being rivalled by a new group. The Rolling Stones were the new kids on the block, having a number three hit with, 'Not Fade Away'.

Access to more popular music was also to come on the radio, in the form of a pirate radio station called Radio Caroline. This was the brainchild of Ronan O'Rahilly, who converted a Danish ferry and began broadcasting off the coast of Felixstowe. It was an all-day show, seven days a week, from 6am to 6pm.

On the 28th of March the opening was conducted by Simon Dee, with the first pre-recorded show being hosted by Chris Moore, playing a wide variety of music.

As Easter was now upon us, it would mean some time off school. During this period, I would go to Old Trafford in order to get some autographs from United players. There were two midweek training sessions a day, 10am-12pm, and 2.30pm- 4pm.

The players were much more accessible than they are today, maybe because they were not such high earners as today's stars. In fact, it was not until 1961 that the maximum weekly wage of £20 was abolished.

Now players were on an average wage of £35 a week, plus crowd bonuses. These bonuses started at an extra pound if the gate was 35,000, rising to £3 when the gate reached 45,000. The United player's bonus for winning the FA Cup last year was £25. This was paid by the Football Association, as United did not pay a bonus at the time.

Wages were not the only thing different from today, the player's diet and lifestyle left a lot to be desired. Many players would smoke cigarettes, although this was not allowed during training hours, and was limited on match days.

The player's pre-match meal would consist of steak and eggs, followed by a nip of whisky, for medicinal purposes. On match days, the Manchester United players would meet at Davyhulme Golf Club, have their meal, then a few of the players would enjoy a game of cards. In fact, four of the players became known as 'The Big Four', these were Brennan, Charlton, Herd and Stiles. This was because wherever United travelled they would always be seen playing cards.

The football season was now nearing the end, and a crucial match for United was an away fixture against top of the table, Liverpool. This game was also significant in that it was my first time watching United play an away game.

My dad took me and our kid on the train to the Anfield Road ground. Upon reaching the ground there were large crowds of people queueing to enter. It came as quite a shock when my dad told us to join the queue, and he would go in a different entrance.

On entering the ground, it soon became evident that we were probably the only two United fans in that section. We were now in the children's pen of Anfield Road, surrounded by hundreds of Liverpool supporters. We managed to keep a low profile until a Liverpool fan noticed our kid's gloves. For on his light brown leveret gloves, he had written the names of United players, Charlton, Best, and Law.

We now thought we were in deep trouble, but fortunately for us Liverpool was cruising and eventually won the game 3-0. So, we came away unscathed and proceeded to go and find my dad at the other end of the ground.

The Liverpool game was also a significant chapter in the career of George Best. For it was the beginning of a run of games that would astound the footballers of today. So, before they complain of playing too many games, it would be worth taking a look at the competitive games that George played in the month of April 1964. He was to play eleven games which were as follows: -

1. 4th Liverpool. League match.
2. 6th Aston Villa. League match.
3. 8th Manchester City. FA Youth Cup, Semi Final, 1st Leg.
4. 13th Sheffield United. League match.
5. 15th Wales. Northern Ireland debut.
6. 18th Stoke City. League match.
7. 20th Manchester City. FA Youth Cup, 2nd Leg.
8. 25th Nottingham Forest. League match.
9. 27th Swindon Town. Youth Cup Final, 1st Leg
10. 29th Uruguay. Northern Ireland friendly match.
11. 30th Swindon Town. FA Youth Cup Final, 2nd Leg.

This number of games would be unheard of in today's game, but as manager Matt Busby would say, 'It is all part of a footballer's career, and George would benefit from it.'

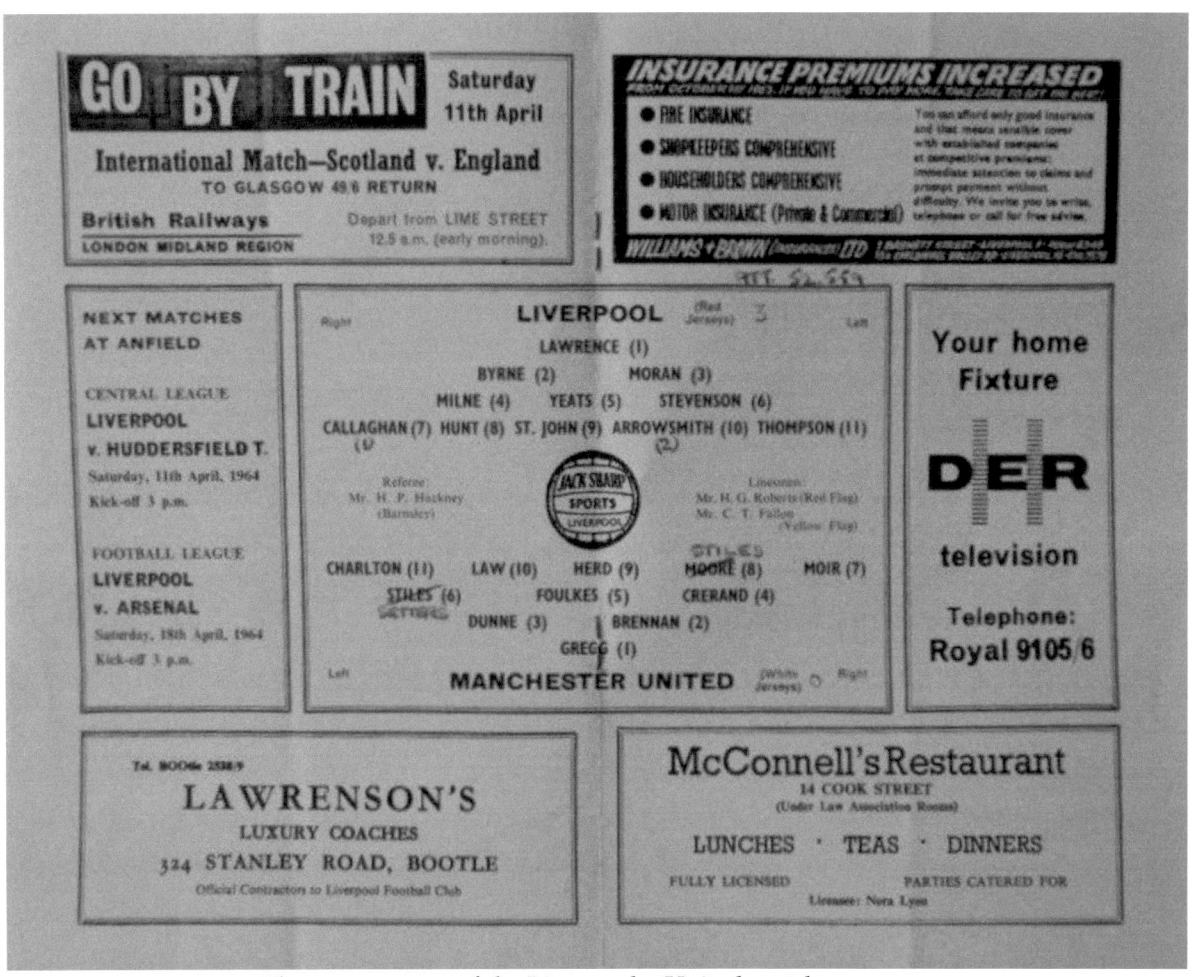

The centre pages of the Liverpool v United match programme.
Score, goal scorers, and attendance are noted.

Of course, seventeen-year-old George was a very important player in Matt Busby's plans for the future. For he was part of a very talented Manchester United Youth team. Apart from George the team contained many players destined for first team football.

Upon beating Swindon Town in that year's FA Youth Cup Final, they had now become the most successful team since 1957. At that time United had won the cup for the fifth time on the run, which were the first five years of the competition.

But this year's competition would be remembered more for United's two-legged semi-final clash with neighbours Manchester City. These two games would be watched by approximately 50,000 adoring fans.

As Manchester City were now in the second division, there would be no first team derby match for the first time since 1949. This greatly increased the interest in the matches, and the fans were not disappointed.

The first leg tie was a particular fiercely contested affair. In a game that United won 4-1, there would be a call for a calmer approach from both sides for the second leg.

City were confident of reversing the score in the second leg, as they thought the score-line did not reflect how close the two teams were. But it was not to be as United triumphed 4-3, making the aggregate score 8-4 in their favour.

It was evident from these two games that both sides contained many talented players. That was to prove correct, as at least eight players from each team would go on to play first team football.

These young footballers were not the high earners of today's counterparts. Earning on average, seven pounds a week, their income was supplemented with luncheon vouchers to buy their meals. These vouchers would normally be used at the UCP on Whitworth Street, in Manchester town centre.

There the United players would meet with the City players and enjoy a three-course meal for around 3/-. After their meal many of the players would go on to the Plaza, which was one of the many music venues of the town centre.

Another music club was called Mr Smiths, where popular artists such as Johnnie Ray and Lonnie Donegan performed. There was also the Oasis Club on Lloyd Street, made famous as The Beatles performed what is believed to be their first live show outside the city of Liverpool.

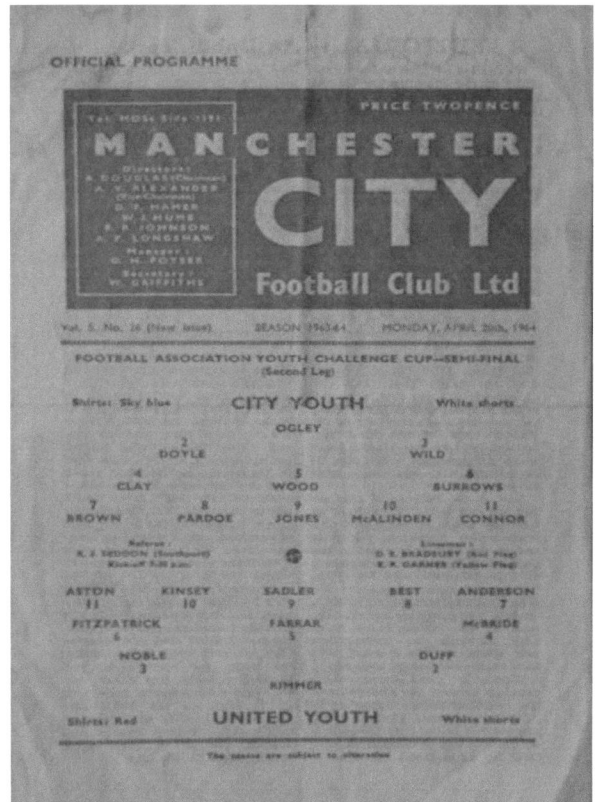
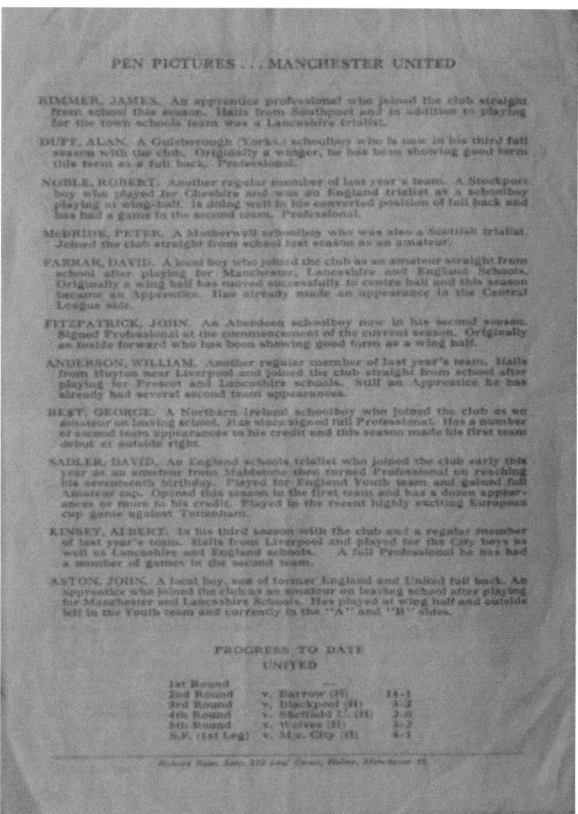

The front and back of the match programme from the 1964 FA Youth Cup Semi Final, second leg.

Undoubtedly the most famous Manchester music venue was the Twisted Wheel, on Brazenose Street, which opened in the January of 1963. The opening night featured The Karl Denver Trio, who would be the first of many famous artists to appear there.

The club provided the opportunity for many local artists to make themselves known to the world. One of these was a former milkman from Moston, Freddie Garrity. He was lead singer with the group Freddie and the Dreamers, who had three top ten hits in 1963. They reached number two in the charts with 'I'm telling you now'.

Other local artists to appear were Wayne Fontana and the Mindbenders, and The Hollies, featuring Salford born Allan Clarke. The first all-nighter at the club featured Spencer Davis, who went on to form the Spencer Davis Group, which included the young and much talented Steve Winwood.

There were many more famous artists to appear at the club, including The Animals, The Kinks, Manfred Mann, Long John Baldry, Georgie Fame and the Blue Flames, The Fourmost. These made the Twisted Wheel an iconic venue in the history of popular music.

The popular music culture was followed with great interest by teenage groups. These fashion-conscious modern-day youngsters loved rhythm and blues, and soul music, and soon acquired the nickname of Mods. Their favoured mode of transport was the motor scooter, usually a Vespa or Lambretta. These scooters were immaculately turned out, adorned with mirrors and badges.

In stark contrast to the Mods, there were Greasers, or Rockers. This group of teenagers were quite the opposite of the Mods. They preferred rock and roll music, they dressed in bicycle leathers and rode around on motor bikes.

With these groups having views entirely the opposite of each other, conflicts would be a common event. Many of these conflicts took place during the holiday season at places such as Brighton and Clacton.

A battle of a different kind was taking place in Salford. The 1st Battalion Lancashire Fusiliers performed an exercise to mark the return of troops from overseas postings. Beginning at the River Irwell on the Crescent, a unit climbed the embankment to overrun supposed terrorists. Then, led by patrol cars they carried on to the Ellor street clearance area. Here a mock confrontation took place with supposed terrorists, using blank ammunition. The exercise was also designed to encourage recruitment.

There is an aerial photograph of the battleground, later in this book.

A group of Mods touring the streets of England. Soon the scooters would be adorned with many mirrors.

The moment had arrived for my favourite event of the year. Our annual family summer holiday was now upon us. One of the perks of my dad working on the railway was that he received free train travel. That meant he could take the whole family to anywhere in Britain.

To maximise the value of this free train pass we would travel as far as possible. Another benefit would be that accommodation was cheaper outside the school holidays. That meant two weeks off school without penalties.

This year we would be holidaying at Ryde, on The Isle of Wight. It would be a long journey by taxi, train and ferry, but that was all part of the holiday. In fact, this was the only time of the year that we would travel by taxi.

So, the adventure began; firstly, a taxi to Manchester Exchange Station, which was actually in Salford. This station was unique in that it had the longest platform in Europe. Platform eleven had enough space for three trains and stretched as far as Manchester Victoria train station.

Travelling by train was a great pleasure. There was an unforgettable odour in the individual compartments from the superbly upholstered seating, leather window blinds, and a thick leather strap to lower the window.

Quite the opposite can be said about the next part of the journey. For upon reaching London, we now had to embark on a traumatic trek across the city. This was by the London underground network at a busy commuter period of the day. There would be a mad rush to get on the trains and we became separated from my mother. We left the train at the next stop, and to our delight my mother was on the next train to arrive.

Fortunately, there were no more hiccups on our journey, and we reached our holiday accommodation. We would be staying in a boarding house, which was common practice at this time. Boarding houses had more of a homely feel than an hotel. We had one bedroom with a sink in the corner, the bathroom was along the landing. The television room was actually the front parlour.

Although only a small island, approximately 150 square miles, the Isle of Wight had lots to offer. There were many sandy beaches, a zoo in Sandown, castles at Carisbrooke and Yarmouth. A visit to The Needles at Alum Bay would be remembered more for the souvenir shop. There you could purchase a glass ornament and fill it with many different coloured sands. For my parents a visit to Osbourne House was a must, as this was once the residence of Queen Victoria. What made the trips even better was that all the places could be reached aboard a steam train which covered the whole island. Again, the train fare would be discounted as my dad worked on the railways. All in all, the Isle of Wight was my most memorable holiday resort, and I would definitely be visiting again.

The early 1960's witnessed many new developments.

Halogen lamps replaced gas powered lamps. Spacewar, the first computer video game was produced. The patent for the first Jacuzzi was filed. The computer mouse, compact audio cassette tapes, push button telephones, fibre tipped pens, and last but not least, Weight Watchers all came to prominence in this era.

For myself, the early 1960's gave me my most memorable childhood experiences while gaining a great number of friends. But undoubtedly a defining moment at that time was the day I watched Manchester United in the 1963 FA Cup Final, my passion then became to watch United whenever possible. They have since given me, my family and friends many hours of entertainment and excitement, which, I am sure, will carry on forever more.

In the News

Muhammad Ali, then known as Cassius Clay, defeated Sonny Liston, to become the World Heavyweight Boxing Champion of the world.

Chapter 11

Salford Redevelopment

With the red of Manchester United now coursing through my veins, I excitedly awaited the upcoming football season.

United had finished in a respectable second position in their previous campaign, and they had high hopes for the 1964-65 season.

During the summer break, they had secured the services of John Connelly from Burnley. Costing £60,000, the England international right winger was considered a bargain buy. With the young George Best on the left wing, the supply line for our strikers now looked complete.

Denis Law and David Herd were our main strike force, both being prolific goal scorers throughout their careers. Bobby Charlton and Pat Crerand would be the linchpins of the midfield area. A solid defence behind them consisted of Tony Dunne, Shay Brennan, Bill Foulkes, Nobby Stiles, and goalkeeper Dave Gaskell.

The season did not get off to the greatest of starts, with only one win in the first five games. Drastic action was called for by the manager, Matt Busby. Matt decided to replace Dave Gaskell with The Irish goalkeeper, Pat Dunne.

This seemed to have the desired effect, as the results gradually improved, and by the end of October, United were top of the League.

In Salford a major housing redevelopment had begun. The Ellor Street area was to be transformed, with new high-rise tower blocks replacing the rows of terraced houses. The new flats would be made of prefabricated concrete sections. These sections would be factory- made and then transported to site and could be erected as quickly as one floor a week.

The first block to be completed was called Walter Greenwood Court, which stood until the new millennium. This type of housing was a stark contrast to the old 'Hanky Park' housing development.

It was not only the houses that were being redeveloped; our roads were also undergoing extensive work. The Crescent, part of the A6 road had been widened to three lanes in both directions. It was hoped that this would ease traffic congestion, this being the main road into Manchester town centre.

While all this work was going on an unusual phenomenon took place in Salford. A small tornado, or gustnado, swept through the City causing damage to buildings in its path.

The January of 1965 was also the time for a major announcement in the football world. Stoke City footballer, Stanley Matthews, nicknamed 'The Wizard of the Dribble' was knighted for his services to football. He was the first player to receive this honour while still playing as a professional footballer.

Unfortunately, this season would witness his last Football League game. He was finding it increasingly hard to break into the first team. It would be just after his 50th Birthday that Sir Stanley did manage to play his only first team game of the season.

That game against Fulham would be his last Football League game, incidentally, Stoke City won, 3-1.

Another local road that was undergoing some reconstruction was the section of the A6 around the historic Woolpack Hotel, Pendleton. This was one of the last public houses to have a working horse trough in situ.

But it was now the time for the horse trough to be rehomed. After much discussion it was decided that it should go to Broughton High School, to be used as a garden ornament.

A few hundred yards from the Woolpack stood the Ambassador Cinema, which had been undergoing extensive refurbishment. On reopening it would no longer be a cinema, but a bingo hall.

The opening ceremony was conducted by Violet Carson, famous for playing Ena Sharples in Coronation Street. This was quite fitting, as Violet once played the piano during the interludes at this cinema.

The end of the 'Ambass' as a cinema meant that there were only four cinemas left in Salford. Whereas twelve years ago there were twenty-one.

As the football season was drawing to a close, there was a three-way tussle for the 1st Division Championship. Manchester United, Chelsea, and Leeds United were the teams involved.

In the middle of April Manchester United went top of the league, and never looked back. They won the title on goal difference, from second placed Leeds United.

John Connelly had proved to be a useful addition to the team. As well as providing many assists, he weighed in with 15 league goals. Denis Law and David Herd were the main goal scorers, with 48 goals between them.

The extended season also saw Manchester United reach the semi-final stage of the Inter Cities Fairs Cup. Although they lost the match against Hungarian side, Ferencvaros.

Salford Crescent

The photograph above shows Salford Crescent before it was widened. There were only two lanes for traffic, and quite a wide pavement.

Quite extensive work was required to transform the road into a six-lane highway. This can be seen in this excellent photograph. The road needed to be extended out towards the River Irwell.

These two photographs show the road reconstruction when it was completed. There are now three lanes of traffic in either direction. On the left the River Irwell meanders past the floral display for the City of Salford. In the far background can be seen the CIS Building. In the near background are Salford Royal Hospital, St Phillips Church, and Salford Cathedral.

The famous artist, LS Lowry was made an Honorary Freeman of the City of Salford. He had lived and worked in the city for four decades. Much inspiration for his works was gained from the industrial buildings in the city.

The people in his drawings and paintings resembled stick figures. Hence the phrase; 'Matchstalk Men and Matchstalk Cats and Dogs'. This would be the title of a number one hit song by Brian and Michael.

Today there are buildings in his name, such as The Lowry Theatre and Art Gallery, the Lowry Shopping Outlet, and the Lowry Hotel.

Many years ago, the streets of Salford were predominantly lit by gaslight. There were thousands of these lights, which all be lit individually by hand. The people who lit them became known as stickmen. Now that it was time for the last of these stickmen to retire. Therefore, it was decided that the last forty gas lights would be put out of use.

On the entertainment scene, The Beatles were smashing it in America. Their concert at New York's Shea Stadium attracted 56,000 fans.

Not so good though, for Bob Dylan. He was booed off stage because he had played an electric guitar. His fans saw this as a betrayal to folk music.

In the fashion world a new clothing item burst onto the scene. This was the mini skirt, brought into prominence by fashion designer, Mary Quant. The mini skirt had the added benefit of avoiding purchase tax. This was because the mini skirt length was less than twenty-four inches, so it would be classed as children's wear.

Because of health issues associated with cigarette smoking, the Government decided to take action. So, from the 1st of August 1965 they would impose a ban on all cigarette advertising on British television.

On a personal note, my next school term would be my last at primary school. Soon I would be taking the eleven-plus exam. This examination was devised to determine which secondary school students would be best suited to attend.

The exam would test a student's ability to solve certain problems. There would also be questions on Mathematics and English. In many ways it was similar to an IQ test. The marks achieved would determine which type of secondary school you would attend next.

By adopting the Tripartite System there would be three types of secondary schools available for the next stage of education. Students with high pass marks would go to a Grammar School. A pass, with lower marks would mean that you would go to a Technical School. Secondary Modern Schools were available to all others.

Because of the marks I achieved, my next school would be Salford Technical High School. This type of school is aimed at developing your technical abilities. Hopefully I will go on to gain an apprenticeship in a trade.

On hearing that I had passed the exam, my parents and teacher, Mr Vernon, were over the moon. Personally, I would have much preferred to have gone with all my school friends to Clarendon Secondary Modern School.

But I could not disappoint my parents and teacher, so my next school would be 'Salford Tech'.

The city of Salford became the first in the country to use a pioneering technique in the car wash industry. Weaste Service Station, on Eccles New Road opened a five-minute car wash system.

With 1966 now upon us, this would be a monumental year for English football. England would be hosting the Football World Cup. The teams would be playing for, the now named, Jules Rimet Trophy. But there was to be a slight problem. Whilst being displayed in the Westminster Hall, London, the trophy was stolen.

A week passed by, without any sign of the trophy. Then miraculously it was found in a garden hedge, by a dog. The dog, named Pickles, became an overnight sensation. He was awarded a medal, by the National Canine Defence League.

The collie became a TV celebrity, and even appeared in film. The film was called 'The Spy with a Cold Nose', and starred the comedian, Eric Sykes.

Locally one of Cross Lane's oldest buildings was to be demolished. The Windsor Building was built in the 1790s and now owned by Hall's Hygiene Company. Originally founded in America, it was now Salford's oldest herbalist.

It would be the case of out with the old, and in with the new. This was because The Willows Social Club would be opening at Salford Rugby League Club. It would later incorporate a lounge/bar room, function rooms, and a variety venue. It was planned for the best variety acts from throughout the world to appear there.

Salford Docks were also set to acquire something new. The last of their steam trains were being replaced with diesel shunting engines. Built by Rolls Royce, these engines would increase the fleet to thirty-five, with a total cost of around £500,000.

On a sombre note, the most evil pair of people in Britain were sentenced to life in prison. Ian Brady and Myra Hindley dubbed 'The Moors Murderers', murdered five children, and buried their bodies on Saddleworth Moor.

It was now time for the 1966 FIFA World Cup to begin. This particular World Cup would make two animals famous throughout the world. Firstly, there was Pickles the dog, as mentioned earlier.

The second animal was a lion named World Cup Willie. Although a cartoon character, he became the first-ever World Cup mascot. Incidentally, if you visit the National Football Museum in Manchester, on display there is replica of the Jules Rimet Trophy and Pickle's dog collar.

There was a bit of controversy surrounding the tournament when it was boycotted by all of the African nations. This was because of a disagreement with the qualifying rules.

England, managed by Alf Ramsey started the tournament second favourites behind Brazil. In the group stages England played Uruguay, Mexico and France. They finished top of the group, without conceding a goal. There would be a shock in group four, where newcomers, North Korea beat Italy 1-0 and qualified from their group.

England's quarter-final opponents were Argentina. In an ill-tempered encounter, England won the game 1-0. Still having not conceded a goal, they would now play Portugal in the semi-final.

Portugal had the player of the tournament, Eusebio, in their team. Nicknamed 'The Black Pearl', he was the tournament's top goal scorer so far with seven goals. But we had someone better, in Bobby Charlton. He scored both our goals, in a 2-1 win.

England would now play West Germany in the final at Wembley Stadium in front of 98,000 fans. Despite going a goal behind, England eventually triumphed 4-2 after extra time.

Towards the end of extra time, with England leading 3-2 some fans began invading the pitch. BBC match commentator, Kenneth Wolstenholme said 'Some people are on the pitch, they think it's all over, (Geoff Hurst scored England's forth goal) it is now'. A sentence immortalised to this day.

This was the last World Cup Final to be broadcast in black and white. Although colour was added later, and it could be watched at the cinema.

After the summer holidays it was time for me to attend my new secondary school. I only knew one other pupil at the school, and he was two years above me.

Wearing a school uniform was alien to me, as none of my friends wore one. We were also told to use a briefcase for our school items, but I got away with using a haversack.

Initially I found the schoolwork quite hard, plus we were given a lot of homework. But I soon got used to the workload and settled in with my new schoolmates.

My old school, New Windsor, came under a compulsory purchase order. It would soon be demolished to make way for redevelopment.

On the 21st of October 1966, tragedy hit the Welsh village of Aberfan. A coal tip overlooking the village slid down, engulfing the primary school and nearby houses. 144 people died, 116 of them being children.

World Cup Willie 1966

Two souvenirs from the 1966 World Cup. A Watney Mann Ale glass, and a World Cup Willie rolykin.

Chapter 12

One giant leap for mankind

My first term at Salford Technical High School was now well under way. I was delighted to find that the school put a great emphasis on physical education. We even had our own tennis courts and swimming baths, which was quite rare.

Having our own swimming baths gave us a lot more opportunities to gain our swimming proficiency certificates. These included swimming various distances and lifesaving. A part of the tests required you to swim to the bottom of the pool to retrieve a rubber brick, this being in the deep end of the pool.

But the test I found the most difficult was when I had to swim whilst waring my pyjamas, as they become very heavy when wet.

Although it was good to have the baths on our doorstep, it was sad to hear of the closing of Pendleton Baths. As that was where I learnt to swim. The good news however was there would be a new swimming baths opening in Salford, the first since 1910.Named Broughton Baths, it is still used to this day.

In the March of 1967, our coastal areas were the hub of activity. The first ever North Sea gas came ashore at Easington, in the East Riding of Yorkshire.

Two weeks later the super tanker, SS Torrey Canyon ran aground off the southwest coast. This caused the worst ever spill of crude oil into the sea. As a result, wildlife perished along the coastlines of England, France and Spain.

This year the world would see a new country win the Eurovision Song Contest. Yes, for the first time it would be the United Kingdom who won the contest. Sandie Shaw, singing "Puppet on a String" brought home the title.

A new pop group burst on to the scene this year. Recording their debut album were, The Bee Gees.

Now if you decided to buy this album, you may have thought to go to an ATM and withdraw some money out. Well, you would be in luck, if you lived in Enfield. This was because Barclays Bank, Enfield, had just become the first ATM to be used worldwide. The first transaction was made by the actor and comedian, Reg Varney.

British football was given a boost when Glasgow Celtic became their first winners of the European Cup.

My team, Manchester United were also having success in their league campaign. Once again it was the change of goalkeeper, early in the season that proved a deciding factor.

Alex Stepney was signed from Chelsea for £55,000. After making his debut against Manchester City he played in all the remaining league games.

Another significant change was young John Aston replacing John Connelly on the wing. John then left to join Blackburn Rovers in the second division.

There were also a few games played by the talented youngsters, David Sadler and Bobby Noble. They would replace David Herd and Shay Brennan for some of the season.

These team changes were to prove a success. United went on to win the first division title, four points clear of Nottingham Forest. Little did anybody know, but this would be United's last league title for twenty-six more years.

I was now in my second term at Salford Technical High School, and I was looking forward to a planned school trip.

The destination was Westward Ho in the south of England.

But unfortunately, the trip was cancelled. This was because of an outbreak of foot and mouth disease. The disease was highly contagious which resulted in the slaughter of almost half a million cattle.

The foot and mouth disease was also having a negative effect on our turf accountants, now better known as bookmakers. But not so for a pair of Salford entrepreneurs.

Fred and Peter Done had recently opened their first betting shop in Salford, named Done Brothers. This venture was partly financed with money won by betting on England to win the World Cup in the previous year.

While many bookmakers were going out of business, Done Brothers pivoted from horse racing to greyhound racing in order to keep the business running.

During the following years the business expanded and changed its name to Betfred. Today a lot of their business is done on the internet. But they still have over 1,600 shops and have a turnover of over £10 billion.

Towards the end of 1967 there was a major breakthrough in the medical world. Surgeon, Christian Barnard performed the world's first ever heart transplant.

After 176 years of independent operation 1968 saw the merger of Salford and Manchester police forces.

In the preceding years Salford police force had been credited with many new innovations. These included play streets, police telephone boxes, fog flares, and the distinctive white coats, which were sometimes required for their force.

Above. Children are helped across the road by a policeman, wearing a distinctive white coat. This was on the busy A6 road, Chapel Street, Salford. Salford Cathedral is on the left of the photograph, taken in 1931.

Below. Again, the white coat is evident on this foggy street scene. It can be seen that the fog flare is connected to the gas main under the grid below.

Across the Atlantic Ocean, The USA would witness the assassination of two major political figures. First of all, there was the shooting of Doctor Martin Luther King, who was the leader of the Civil Rights movement.

His funeral, in Atlanta, was attended by over 150,000 people. But the murder triggered widespread violence across America. His killer would eventually be arrested in London.

The second assassination was of Senator Robert Kennedy, brother of the late John Kennedy. He was gunned down by a young Palestinian, because of his support for Israel.

Manchester United were aiming for success in the European Cup. Now, ten years after the Munich tragedy, they were in prime position to win the trophy.

A new young striker had emerged through the ranks this season. Collyhurst born, Brian Kidd became a regular first team player. The eighteen-year-old, looked to have a bright future ahead of him.

In the early rounds, United would beat Hibernian of Malta, Sarajevo of Yugoslavia, and Gornik Zabrze of Poland.

In the semi- final they would meet the mighty Real Madrid of Spain.

Tickets for the first leg at Old Trafford were hard to obtain. I finally managed to get one and made one of my rare visits to the Scoreboard End. I would usually stand in the Stretford End, as the atmosphere was much better. United won the game 1-0, thanks to a goal from George Best.

This set up the second leg to be a make-or-break game for the Red Devils. Despite going behind, United eventually drew the game 3-3 to progress to the final.

The final took place at Wembley Stadium, on the 29th of May 1968 against Benfica of Portugal. United, in a changed strip of all blue, would have to try and stop their star player, Eusebio.

With a few minutes of normal time remaining, and the score at 1-1, Eusebio was through with only the goalkeeper to beat. But Alex Stepney rose to the challenge and brought off a magnificent save.

After extra time United triumphed 4-1. The United scorers were Bobby Charlton 2, George Best, and Brian Kidd, who was also celebrating his 19th birthday.

Locally we would see the end of another cinema. Whilst in the process of refurbishment, The Kings, on Regent Road was completely destroyed by fire and never reopened.

This year also witnessed the end of a 138-year love affair with the steam engine. Passengers were hauled by a steam locomotive for the last time on 11th August 1968. They travelled from Liverpool to Carlisle and back on the train, nicknamed "The Fifteen Guinea Special". It was given the nickname because of the high price of the journey, £15-15s, more than double the usual fare.

At the beginning of 1969 there was some surprising news coming from Old Trafford. Manchester United's manager, Sir Matt Busby announced that he would be retiring at the end of the present season.

With United currently sitting sixth from the bottom of the league, and with an ageing team, Matt's successor would have a hard task on his hands.

The man chosen to do the job was 31-year-old, Wilf McGuinness. Wilf was one of the original Busby Babes and was currently employed at the club as youth team manager.

Attending football matches had become, for some people an excuse for violence. A new subculture had developed across England, called "Skinheads".

Skinheads were an offshoot from the Mod culture. They would dress in checked shirts, jeans, and steel toe capped or Dr Marten boots. With this dress code, together with their shaven heads, they resembled a building site worker.

They were notorious for violence, especially at football matches.

No such violence was present at Rugby League matches. My local team, Salford had been assembling some talented players. These included, Dave Watkins, Colin Dixon, Bill Burgess, Mike Coulman, and Chris Hesketh, to name just a few. This year they had booked a place in the Challenge Cup Final, for the first time in 30 years. In a close fought game, they lost to Castleford 6-11. But there were signs of better things to come.

Staying local, the foundations were finally laid for the new Salford Shopping Centre, in the Pendleton area. Some steel work quickly followed, as it looked on schedule for completion in approximately two years' time.

Also, around this period the bus services in this area became integrated in the South Lancashire and Northeast Cheshire, or SELNEC network. The "Sunglow" buses were an intense shade of yellowish orange colour.

Public bus services had their roots in Salford. Back in 1824, Salford toll keeper, John Greenwood started the first horse bus service from Pendleton to Manchester.

One of the first of the "Sunglow" buses, painted in the bright orange colour. This photograph was taken in Manchester's Transport Museum. The museum is home to many types of transport, dating back to 1824.

Across the pond, in America there was a major event in the history of Rock and Roll. This was the Woodstock Music Festival, taking place at a dairy farm in Bethel, New York.

The festival attracted more than 450,000 people, who would watch over 30 performances. A few of the more famous performers were, Jimi Hendrix, Joan Baez, Janis Joplin, and Creedence Clearwater Revival.

One band who could not make it to the festival was The Beatles. But the "Fab Four" made their own news this year, with two of the group getting married. Paul McCartney married Linda Eastman. While John Lennon tied the knot with Yoko Ono, the ceremony taking place in Gibraltar.

The final year of the 1960s would witness an event that would be watched worldwide.

Back in 1961 President John F Kennedy set up an Apollo 11 mission. This mission was to perform a crewed landing on the moon.

On the 16th of July 1969 a Saturn rocket was launched from the Kennedy Space Center., USA. The rocket would power the command module, Columbia and the moon craft, Eagle. The rocket rose up at 24,800 mph, through the earth's atmosphere, towards its destination.

On the 20th of July the moon craft descended onto the moon's surface.

A message then came through to earth, "The Eagle has landed". Four hours later, astronaut Neil Armstrong would become the first person to step onto the moon's surface. Proudly declaring, "That's one small step for a man, one giant leap for mankind". Although the "a" became lost to the ear, because of radio static.

Neil was followed by his colleague, Edwin "Buzz" Aldrin, as they planted the Stars and Stripes flag. The third member of the crew, Michael Collins, remained in the command module orbiting the moon.

A total of 21 hours 36 minutes was spent on the Moon's surface. Various experiments were performed, and samples of lunar materials were collected.

They returned to Earth, and landed in the Pacific Ocean, on the 24th of July 1969.

For many people the Moon landing would define the 1960s. Personally, nothing would ever outshine watching Manchester United in the 1963 FA Cup Final.

An aerial view of the battleground. On the left of the photograph is the covered Market Place and Clarendon School. On the bottom right is The Oliver Heywood monument. The derelict land used for the mock battle would soon be used for a major housing development.

The steam train was a common site in the 1960's. This one is aptly named City of Salford.

Below: Salford Museum and Art Gallery, home of the Salford Local History Library. This is where I carried out much of the research for this book. The assistance from the staff made this book possible, for which I will be eternally grateful.

Above: The original entrance to Manchester Racecourse, Cromwell Road, Salford

Above: - The Woolpack Hotel. Situated at the junction of Eccles Old Road, to the left, and Bolton Road, to the right. In the cobbled road can be seen the tram tracks. Horses would stop outside the Woolpack for a drink of water from the horse trough. This photograph was taken at the beginning of the 20th century

The Woolpack as it looked in the 1960s. To the left of the Woolpack, on Eccles Old Road, there is a petrol station on the land now occupied by Sutton housing.

The road redevelopment begins between Pendleton Church and Salford Shopping Centre.
The three-storey building, top centre, is still there, now apartments.

An aerial view of the completed Salford Shopping Centre. The new road pictured on the previous page can be seen at the top right. The Keystone pub is near the new covered market. SELNEC buses travel on the back road, of what quickly became known as "The Precinct".

Two views of the new road construction. The photographs were taken from a point close to where the old Woolpack once stood. The top photograph is looking towards Pendleton Church. Eccles Old Road is on the right-hand side. On the left-hand side is Bolton Road, and Duchy Road. The bottom photograph shows the opposite direction, with Sutton Flats on the left-hand side.

Above: The, now empty, site of Cross Lane Market. The clock tower and offices still stand. The Cattle Market Pub is on the right, with the public toilets to the left of it. The Craven Heifer Pub stands on the other side of Cross Lane.

Below. The horse trough, which was a feature outside the old Woolpack for many a year. It was eventually donated to Broughton High School, to be used as a garden ornament.

Above. The corner of Cross Lane and Regent Road. The couple with the pram are walking past the Baker's shop on Cross Lane. A little further on is The Church pub, then Disc City.

Below. A view looking up Trafford Road towards Old Trafford. Just out of shot, on the right, behind the grass verge stood the Clowes pub. A little further on is Salford Central Mission, on the corner of Broadway.

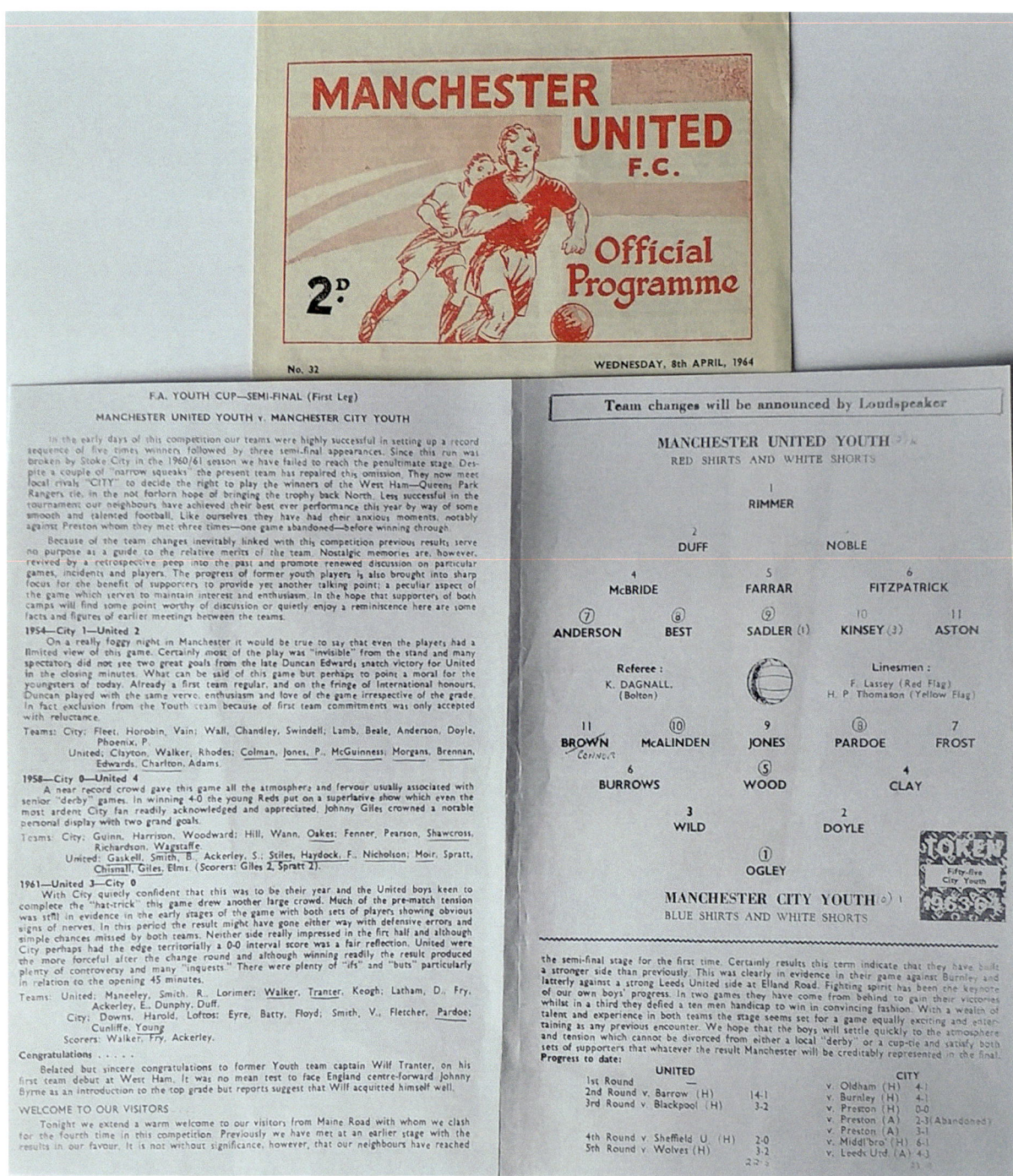

Manchester United v Manchester City Youth Cup Semi-Final 1st leg 1964

The above photograph shows the inside of a four-sided programme from the match between Manchester United and Manchester City. This was the Youth Cup semi-final 1st leg tie on 8th April 1964. In an ill-tempered match, United came out victors, 4-1. The United scorers are marked in brackets, Pardoe scored for City. Also shown is the top section of the front of the programme. Note the price of tuppence

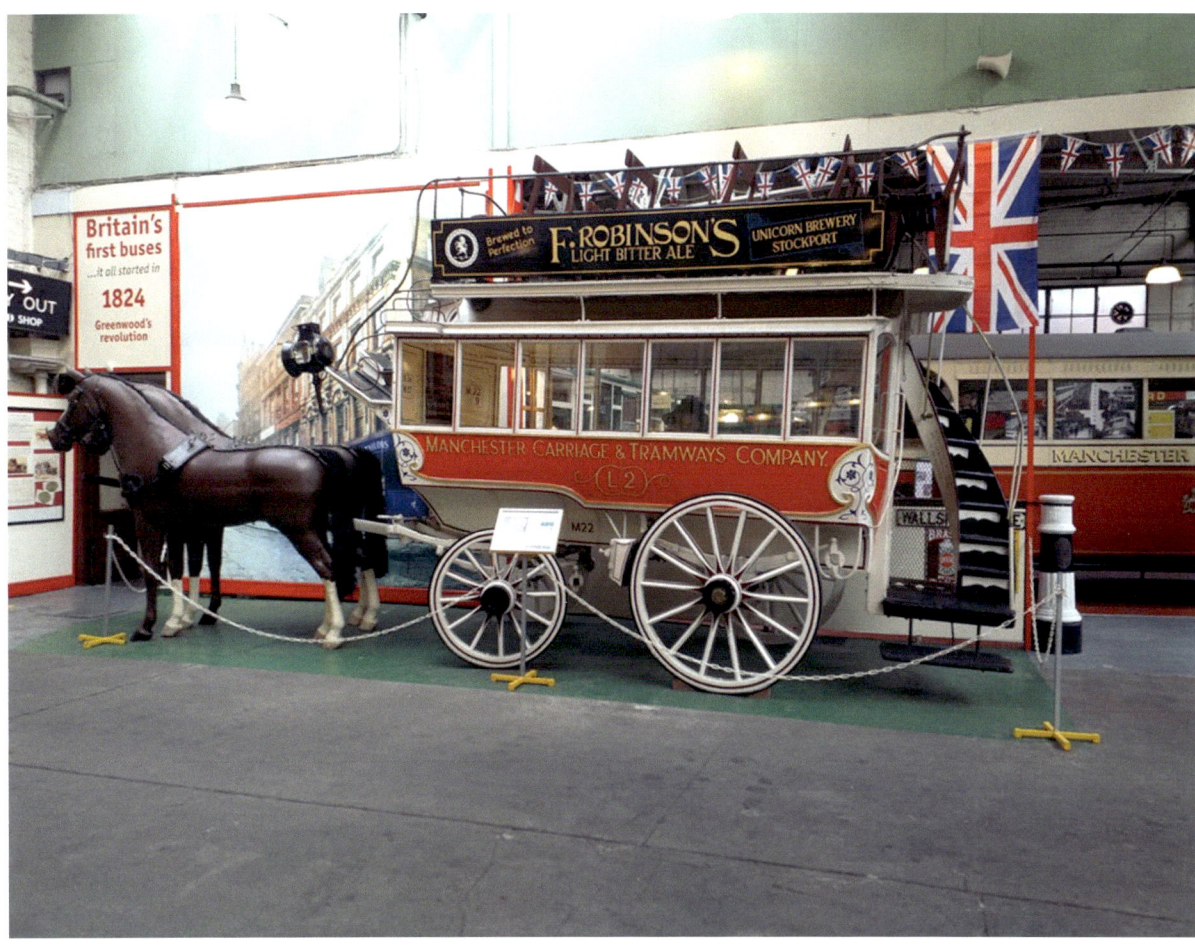

Above. Public bus services had their roots in Salford. This photograph shows John Greenwood's pioneering idea of a horse drawn bus, which first ran from Pendleton to Manchester in 1824.

Below. This is the junction of Cross Lane and Liverpool Street. This 1955 photograph is looking along Liverpool Street towards Manchester. The gasworks can just be seen on the right-hand side.

Acknowledgements

I did eventually revisit The Isle of Wight, some fifty years later. It was everything I expected and more. This time I drove there, thus avoiding the London underground network. I had a great holiday and expected to return there in the future, but I will not leave it as long next time. Researching and then writing this book has given me a great deal of satisfaction. Many events which I had previously forgotten, were reawakened whilst looking into the past.

Much of the research for this book was carried out at the Salford Local History Library on Salford Crescent. There I discovered a mountain of information and old photographs of the Salford area. All of which the library allowed me to include in my book, for this I will be eternally grateful. Another source of information was 'The Theatre of the Mind', better known as the radio. The internet and previous works of literature also proved invaluable in gaining information.

Like many other places, Salford has changed a great deal since the 1960s. Fortunately there are still some iconic buildings still standing. The route I took, when moving house in 1962, can still be followed. Starting at Sacred Trinity Church, The Town Hall Building, Salford Cathedral, The Shouting Soldier, and the Salford Royal Building, all still remain.

Moving on to The Crescent, The Red Dragon public house is still thriving, now named The Crescent. The Police and Fire Stations still stand although empty. More importantly to me is that Salford Museum and Art Gallery still remains, it is now the home of Salford Local History Library.

As we move on to Cross Lane, the Oliver Heywood monument still remains, now situated in the grounds of McDonald's fast-food restaurant. Opposite McDonald's is the building which was once the Fusiliers Public House. Although empty, it is one of the three remaining buildings which were once pubs.

The other two are The Corporation, which is now a fast-food outlet, and The Craven Heifer, which is now a shop. This being the only shop now on Cross Lane, a road which was once a thriving metropolis, now unrecognisable from the 1960's.

As we walk down Cross Lane we reach the junction with Liverpool Street. Looking across the road to the small catchment area where I used to live, there now stands the Post Office sorting building. But glancing to the left across the road can be seen a small section of the original cattle dock wall.

That wall is all that remains of the area from the 1960's. Sadly, that is also all that remains of this book. I hope you enjoyed our trip into the past, and that it rekindled some memories of your own